— • BAKE IT BETTER • —

Would you like to learn to __ a better baker?

We know that so many people watch *The Great British Bake Off* for the tips and techniques you pick up – not only from the judges, but from watching the bakers too. We wanted to distil that knowledge into a library of cookbooks that are specifically designed to take you from novice to expert baker. Individually, each book covers the skills you will want to perfect so that you can master a particular area of baking – everything from cakes to bread, sweet pastries to pies.

We have chosen recipes that are classics of each type, and grouped them together so that they take you on a progression from 'Easy does it' through 'Needs a little skill' to 'Up for a challenge'. Put together, the full series of books will give you a comprehensive collection of the best recipes, along with all the advice you need to become a better baker.

The triumphs and lessons of the bakers in the tent show us that not everything works every time. But I hope that with these books as your guide, we have given you a head start towards baking it better every time!

Linda Collister
Series Editor

THE GREAT BRITISH
BAKE OFF®
-• BAKE IT BETTER •-

PASTRY &
PATISSERIE

Joanna Farrow

HODDER &
STOUGHTON

Contents

BAKE IT BETTER
Baker's Guide

BAKE IT BETTER
Recipes

Easy does it   46

Welcome bakers!

If your goal is to bake the sort of beautiful creations that wouldn't look out of place in a French patisserie window, then you'll find *Bake It Better: Pastry & Patisserie* an invaluable guide to getting you there.

Even if you've never made pastry before, you can start with the 'Easy does it' section and master simple but delicious recipes like Blueberry and Lemon Financiers and Vanilla Chouquettes. Some of the recipes in this section use bought pastry so you can learn key skills such as rolling out and shaping before taking on the more complex 'start from scratch' recipes that follow in the section that 'Needs a little skill'. These are slightly more complex dishes such as a beautiful French Apple Tart and irresistibly glazed Danish Pastries. The more you bake, the sooner you'll be 'Up for a challenge', the final section of recipes that will put your newly acquired baking skills to the test.

The colour strip on the right-hand side of the page tells you at a glance the level of difficulty of the recipe (from one spoon for easy to three spoons for more of a challenge), and gives you a helpful checklist of the skills and special equipment you will use. Before you begin, have a look at the Baker's Guide at the beginning of the book. This will tell you what equipment you need to get started, introduce you to the most important ingredients and explain some terms and techniques for the pastries and skills in more detail.

Pastry and patisserie recipes can be made for any occasion, whether you simply want to serve your family a lovely treat with afternoon tea, or create a showstopping end to a special occasion. Perfect this extensive range of beautiful bakes that will take you well on the way to being a 'star baker'!

HOW TO USE THIS BOOK

SECTION 1: BAKER'S GUIDE
Read this section before you start baking.

The Baker's Guide contains key information on ingredients (pages 10–15), equipment (pages 16–21) and skills (pages 22–41) relevant to the recipes in the book.

Refer back to the Baker's Guide when you're baking if you want a refresher on a particular skill. In the recipes the first mention of each skill is highlighted in bold.

SECTION 2: RECIPES
Colour strips on the right-hand side and 1, 2 or 3 spoons show the level of difficulty of the recipe. Within the colour strips you'll find helpful information to help you decide what to bake: Hands-on time; Hands-off time; Baking time; Makes/Serves; Special equipment; Method used; Storage.

Refer back to the Baker's Guide when a skill is highlighted in bold in the recipe if you need a reminder.

Try Something Different options are given where the recipe lends itself to experimenting with other ingredients or decorations.

BAKE IT BETTER
Baker's Guide

Ingredients

Pastry and patisserie recipes vary hugely in the amount of ingredients required. A simple bake might only require a handful of ingredients but a showstopping gateau will inevitably require more – and sometimes less widely available items. Having the right ingredients to hand before you start baking will start you on the route to success, so do a checklist before you start. The following list will guide you through the key ingredients used in this book.

BAKING POWDER, BICARBONATE OF SODA AND CREAM OF TARTAR

Some cakes require the help of a chemical raising agent to increase their lightness. The two most common raising agents are **bicarbonate of soda** and **cream of tartar**. **Baking powder** is a mixture of both and is the most commonly used in creamed cakes to make them rise. **Whisked sponges** are lightened by beating air into the mixture before baking so they don't require any additional raising agent. Cream of tartar is also used in some **meringue** recipes as it stabilises the egg whites and, as an acid, counteracts the adverse effects of any traces of grease.

BUTTER

Butter gives pastry and patisserie a good texture and rich, moist flavour. Most bakers use **unsalted butter**, which contains less whey than salted butter, producing a more evenly coloured bake. **Slightly salted** butter can be used instead, in which case you won't need to add any extra salt to the recipe. Avoid using regular **salted butter** as this can contain about 2 per cent salt. You can get away with this amount in pastry but the saltiness can be overpowering in cakes and delicate fillings. For most pastries, butter is used chilled, straight from the fridge, but for creamed cakes it's easier to work with it when it is at room temperature, so try to remember to remove it from the fridge in advance. If you forget, it can be softened (very carefully) in the microwave on medium power for a few seconds. Store butter tightly wrapped in its original wrapper in the fridge, away from strong flavours. It also freezes well for up to a month.

Dairy-free spread, a vegetable oil-based alternative to butter, can be used as a substitute for butter in many recipes, particularly sponges and some pastries. Make sure the label states that it's good for baking before you buy.

CHOCOLATE

Good-quality chocolate is widely available in supermarkets and you can buy chips in larger bags from online suppliers, but you can also use bars of chocolate chopped into similar-sized pieces.

Dark chocolate is most widely used in this book. Using one with around 70 per cent cocoa solids will give your bakes the best flavour – anything over 75 per cent can be too dry and bitter for general baking. **Cocoa powder** is a dark, unsweetened powder made from pure cocoa with nearly all the cocoa butter removed – it is very bitter and powerfully flavoured, and can be used to add an excellent, rich chocolate taste to sweet pastry (see Chocolate Maple Tarts with Hazelnut Brittle, page 114). Don't use drinking chocolate instead of cocoa powder; it has had sugar and dried milk powder added to it, so it won't produce the same results.

Store bars of chocolate well wrapped in a cool, dry, dark cupboard, and away from strong-flavoured ingredients as they can affect the chocolate's own flavour. Always make sure that you've chopped your chocolate before you melt it, to ensure that it melts quickly and evenly, whether you're making a ganache (see Black Forest Meringues, page 78) or melting in a bain-marie (see Chocolate Mont Blanc Cups, page 156).

CREAM

Make sure to use the type of cream recommended in the recipe – the fat contents vary a lot and will affect whether a sauce thickens properly, a custard sets or the cream will whip. For best results, chill cream thoroughly before whipping (see page 39).

Single cream contains 18 per cent butterfat and is good for pouring over pastries to serve and adding to fillings, but it cannot be whipped.

Whipping cream contains at least 35 per cent butterfat and whips well without being overly rich.

Double cream contains at least 48 per cent butterfat. It also whips well, producing a richer flavour than whipping cream. Take care when whipping double cream as it will over-thicken easily and the texture will spoil.

Crème fraîche is French soured cream. It has a creamy but tangy flavour and cannot be whipped. It's better used for serving as an accompaniment to fruit, nut or chocolate tarts and pastries.

Soured cream has only around 18 per cent butterfat and is made by introducing a bacterial culture to give it a naturally 'soured' tang. It is used in this book in a number of pastries, to give a crisp, flaky texture to a simple rubbed-in pastry (see Mini Pissaladières, page 62, and Apple and Lemon Treacle Tart, page 96).

EGGS

Eggs are used to create volume and flavour in sponge and whisked cakes and to enrich pastry. In patisserie the yolks and whites are often used separately. Yolks are used to enrich custards and **pâte sucrée**, while the whites form the basis of **meringues**.

All the recipes in this book use medium-sized eggs, each weighing about 62–65g. It's important to use the correct weight of egg so you have the right amount in relation to the other weighed ingredients in your recipe. Too little egg and a sponge might not rise properly; too much and a pastry might be too soft and collapse as it cooks.

Store eggs in the main body of the fridge in the box you bought them in. This will give you an 'at-a-glance' guide to their best-before date. The box also protects the shells and prevents them from absorbing strong flavours from other items in the fridge. They're purposely packed pointed ends down to protect and centre the yolk so it doesn't dry out.

Eggs are best used at room temperature for baking as they give a greater volume on beating (see page 29). It's not a big problem if you forget to remove them in advance, as the recipe will still work but it's a good idea to get them out of the fridge 30–60 minutes before you use them. If you forget, you might just want to pop them in a bowl of lukewarm water for a few minutes before you start.

Spare egg whites will keep for 3–4 days in the fridge in a sealed container, or for up to 1 month in the freezer. Label them with the date and quantity, and always defrost thoroughly before using. Egg yolks cannot be frozen.

EXTRACTS AND FLAVOURINGS
Try to avoid the synthetic versions of flavourings wherever possible, as these can give your bake a rather unpleasant 'fake' taste.

Vanilla is the most commonly used flavouring in patisserie. It is worth paying a little bit more for the 'extract', rather than a cheaper 'essence' which might be made from artificial flavourings.

Vanilla bean paste is made from the seeds of the vanilla pod and provides an even more concentrated flavour than vanilla extract. Top of the range is the **vanilla pod**. The tiny black seeds are scraped from the pods to impart their flavours into creams and fillings such as crème patissière, and once used you can dry them off and pop them into a jar of caster sugar to make **vanilla sugar**.

Ground spices should be measured carefully and kept in screw-topped jars. Use them when they are fresh and within a few months of opening.

Alcohol, in the form of liqueurs or brandies, is used occasionally in pastry and patisserie recipes to flavour fillings or fruit syrups, as in the Savarin with Clementines and Figs (see page 152).

Orange and lemon zest is used in a number of bakes, from the Blueberry and Lemon Financiers on page 60 to the Cardamom and Orange Baklava on page 162 – make sure to always use unwaxed fruit when zesting.

FLOUR
For best baking results, always use fresh flour and aim to use it up well within its best before date. Store unopened packages of flour as they are, but transfer the flour, still in its packaging for easy identification, to a plastic food box, plastic food bag or an airtight storage jar once it has been opened. Make sure you use up old flour before starting on a new pack and don't mix old with new.

Wheat flours are the most commonly used flours in pastry and patisserie. **Plain flour** has had nothing added and is generally used for pastry, whereas **self-raising flour** has baking powder added and is used in sponge cakes where you want the cake to rise. If you run out of self-raising flour, you can make your own by adding 4 teaspoons baking powder to every 225g plain flour, sifting the two together a couple of times for even distribution of the baking powder. These flours are known as 'soft' or 'cake' flours, meaning that they contain a low proportion of gluten to starch.

Strong flour, on the other hand, has a higher proportion of protein to starch than flour used for making cakes. It's the protein content that is key when making yeasted breads: as the dough is kneaded, the protein develops into strands of gluten, which help the dough rise by expanding around the gases produced by the active yeast. Strong flour (sometimes labelled 'bread flour') is used mainly for bread making including croissants, Danish pastries and Savarin (see pages 138, 142 and 152), but it is also good for **rough puff** and **puff pastry**, as it has more elasticity which helps create that all-important extra flakiness.

Gluten-free flours are wheat-free flours that can be used instead of regular flour in both cake and pastry recipes. They are usually made from a combination of rice, potato, tapioca, maize, chickpea, broad bean, white sorgum or buckwheat flours and vary in taste and texture from brand to brand, so it's worth trying a few different ones. If you use gluten-free flour you may need to add xanthan gum to improve the texture of pastry. Check the packet and if your flour doesn't include it already, add 1 teaspoon xanthan gum per 150g flour.

Gluten-free flours tend to need a little more liquid than wheat flours, so they can't always be used exactly as wheat flours in a recipe, but there will usually be some instructions on the packet for further guidance on how to use them.

NUTS

Nuts are best bought in small quantities as their high oil content makes them deteriorate quickly and turn rancid. Store them in airtight containers in a cool, dark place and try to use them up well before their best before date. Some recipes call for 'blanched' nuts. This usually applies to almonds and hazelnuts and means that the dark papery skin covering the nuts has been removed. To blanch hazelnuts at home, scatter them on a baking tray and toast in a medium oven for about 5 minutes. Tip onto a clean tea towel and rub vigorously to remove the skins. The skins of almonds are easiest to remove if soaked in boiling water for 2 minutes to soften, then drained and plunged into cold water before peeling the skins away.

Almonds are the most versatile of all the nuts, used extensively in tart fillings, frangipane, marzipan and praline. If a recipe calls for ground almonds you can go the extra mile by grinding whole blanched almonds in a food-processor for a really full flavour. If you don't have time, bought ground almonds are perfectly acceptable.

Hazelnuts can be used to make brittle or toasted and ground to make hazelnut **pâte sucrée**, as in the Chocolate Maple Tarts with Hazelnut Brittle (see page 114).

Walnuts and pecan nuts are generally interchangeable in baking for their similar appearance and texture. Pecan nuts are slightly sweeter and less bitter.

Pistachio nuts are usually sold with their papery skins attached. Skinned, they reveal a beautiful, deep green nut that contributes a fabulous colour to recipes such as the Chocolate Pistachio Gateau (see page 176). Soak in boiling water for 1 minute, drain and rub in a clean tea towel to loosen the skins. You'll most likely need to finish this process by hand, as some of the skins may stubbornly cling to the nuts.

SUGAR

Sugar does not have a best before or sell by date because it keeps indefinitely if stored in the right conditions. Keep in its packaging or transfer to an airtight container and store in a cool, dry place.

Generally the darker the sugar the more flavour it has. Different sugars combine with other ingredients in different ways, which may affect the end result, so it's best to stick to the type of sugar recommended in the recipe.

Refined **caster sugar** is pure white and is used extensively in pastry and patisserie where sweetness is required but the colour must be left untainted. It has fine grains, which break down easily when beaten with butter and combine well with other ingredients. Crisp white meringues, creamy custards, fruit fillings and delicate sponges all require refined caster sugar. Unrefined **golden caster sugar** has a better flavour and slightly caramelly nuttiness, and is best used when colour is not an issue. **Granulated sugar** has bigger grains and takes longer to dissolve, so is less suitable for cake mixtures or meringues. Both caster and granulated sugar can be used when making sugar syrups and caramel (see page 40), though caster sugar is the more usual choice as it dissolves more quickly and evenly.

Icing sugar is available both as refined (white) and unrefined (golden). Again, the unrefined version has a caramelly colour, so is used less often when a light dusting of white icing sugar is needed to finish a pastry or patisserie. Icing sugar can also be used as a glaze (see page 37). These days, freshly bought icing sugar does not need sifting but it still might 'cake' down a bit during storage, in which case, press it through a sieve before using.

Brown muscovado sugars are available in light and dark. These, along with **demerara sugar**, add a stronger caramel taste and darker colour to your bakes, but they also tend to make them slightly more moist and heavy. They work particularly well in recipes using chocolate and spicy flavours. They may form into lumps during storage, so you'll need to press out the lumps with the back of a metal spoon before using.

Equipment

Patisserie is renowned for supposedly requiring lots of specialist kit. In fact there's very little you need to get started and the average kitchen cupboard contains most of the essentials. There are a few tins you might want to get to make some of the easier recipes such as the Lemon Thyme Madeleines (see page 68) and individual tartlets but you won't need these from the outset. You can collect any other bits of kit required as you delve into the more challenging recipes. Read the equipment list alongside each recipe carefully before you start, to make sure you have everything you need.

BAKING BEANS

Ceramic baking beans are used when baking blind (see page 36) to keep pastry bases flat and the sides upright. If you don't want to go to the expense of buying baking beans just yet, use uncooked rice or dried beans and label them in a jar for this purpose. Like the ceramic baking beans they can be used repeatedly.

BAKING PAPER AND LINERS

Baking paper and liners help you remove cakes and pastries easily from their tins and stop them sticking. **Non-stick baking paper** is a good all-round paper, ideal for lining tins and baking sheets, and for **blind baking**. **Greaseproof paper** is good for wrapping bakes but is not as sturdy as baking paper and doesn't stand up well to heating. **Re-usable silicone liners** are excellent for lining baking sheets and can also be cut to fit other tins you use regularly. Most of the recipes in this book require baking paper, particularly for lining baking sheets. You can easily use the re-usable liners instead – simply wipe them clean after use and store, preferably rolled to prevent creasing, until the next baking session.

BAKING SHEETS AND TRAYS

A **baking sheet** is flat with one raised edge for gripping. A **baking tray** has a shallow raised edge all the way round. Most of the recipes in this book use a baking sheet. It's ideal for meringues, macarons, tarts and recipes where it's easier to slide a cake or pastry from the sheet onto a cooling rack or surface. A firm, sturdy baking sheet that doesn't flex is best for baking as it won't buckle or lose its shape in a hot oven. A bent baking sheet could result in a cracked pastry or spilt filling.

BAKING TINS

It's very important to use the tin that's specified in the recipe. Use one that's too small and the mixture may well spill over the top or sink in the middle. A tin that's too large might produce biscuity, dry results. It's always worth buying solid, heavy-duty tins as these won't lose their shape and will last for ever if properly looked after. After use, always clean and thoroughly dry tins before packing them away.

Springclip tins have a spring release on the side so they are really useful when making more fragile cakes, such as the Cardamom and Orange Baklava and Chocolate Pistachio Gateau (see pages 162 and 176), as the sides can be removed easily without fear of damaging the cake. They come in many sizes, but 18–20cm and 23cm are the most frequently used.

Specialist tins are used for some of the recipes in this book. These are usually fairly expensive so only worth buying if you know you'll make good use of them. They're also very specific shapes and don't easily adapt to other recipes – another reason to be sure before you buy. These tins include **madeleine mould trays, barquette tins, cream horn moulds** and **savarin moulds**. After use, clean thoroughly (not all are dishwasher-proof) and make sure they're completely dry before storing.

Tart and tartlet tins are used in a number of pastry and patisserie recipes in this book; check the recipe carefully to check what size and depth you need as this is usually key to the success of the recipe (see English Maids of Honour Tart on page 84). Metal **tart tins** are best as they're good conductors of heat and give a professional-looking result. Look for a non-stick sturdy metal, such as silver anodised, which will wear well and is easy to clean. Loose-bottomed tins make it easier to remove your finished bake, such as the Apple and Lemon Treacle Tart (see page 96). **Tartlet tins** should also have loose bottoms and the same qualities as large tins; like the large tins they vary considerably in diameter and depth. A 10cm width is a useful size for individual servings. Some small bakes such as Portuguese Custard Tarts (see page 72) and Mini Victoria Sandwich Cakes with Tropical Fruits (see page 74) are baked in the sections of a **muffin tray**, which is a useful, multipurpose piece of equipment. Choose non-stick if available.

BOWLS

It's useful to have a selection of different types of mixing bowls, preferably in an assortment of sizes so you can stack them together for storage. There are pros and cons to the different types. **Heatproof glass** bowls are the best all-purpose choice for mixing, whisking and melting chocolate over a pan of gently simmering water. They're also microwave-proof. **Stainless steel** bowls are lightweight, unbreakable, durable and dishwasher-proof, but they cannot be used in the microwave. **Ceramic** bowls are more attractive but are heavy and crack or break more easily. **Anodised aluminium** bowls are very durable and will last a lifetime, but aren't suitable for the microwave. **Plastic** bowls are all-purpose and cheap and sometimes come with a non-slip rubber base. Bear in mind that you can stabilise any bowl that wobbles on the work surface by folding a damp cloth underneath.

COOLING RACKS

A large wire cooling rack allows air to circulate around a cooling pastry or cake, helping to avoid the dreaded 'soggy bottom'. You can improvise with a wire grill-pan rack, but the finer wires on a cooling rack are more effective.

FOOD-PROCESSOR

A food-processor makes light work of mixing doughs and pastes and finely chopping nuts and other ingredients. Pastries, including **choux pastry** and **pâte sucrée** can be made quickly and efficiently in a food-processor. The recipes in this book focus on making these by hand to develop and master the necessary skills but a food-processor can often be used if time is short (see pages 29 and 34).

KNIVES

The better the knife, the easier you'll find it to perfect your knife skills – and save quite a lot of time too. Knives are made from different materials such as stainless steel and carbon steel. Use ones that you can sharpen or have them sharpened professionally. For pastry and patisserie work a **large, sturdy knife** is good for neat slicing and chopping nuts and fruit. A **small, sharp knife** is useful and good for accurate decorative pastry work. A **long-bladed serrated bread knife** is good for slicing cakes into layers for sandwiching with fillings. A palette knife is useful for lifting pastries and decorations without damaging them, and for spreading icings and fillings. An **off-set palette knife** (one with a kink near the handle end of the blade) is essential for spreading icings smoothly inside a case or anywhere where your fist might be too close to the mixture if spread with a regular palette knife. Over time you might find it useful to collect palette knives in two or three different sizes for large and small-scale patisserie work.

LARGE METAL SPOON
A large metal spoon with a long handle is useful for **folding in** (see page 39) and for transferring cake mixtures, icings and fillings.

MEASURING JUG
Pick a heat-resistant and microwave-safe jug that provides both metric and imperial measures, starting from 50ml and going up to 2 litres. A small measuring jug gives a more accurate measurement for smaller quantities of liquid. When measuring liquids, bend down slightly so you can view the gauge horizontally for better accuracy.

MEASURING SPOONS
A set of measuring spoons is one of the most essential pieces of equipment, as baking is an exact science and everyday teaspoons, dessertspoons and tablespoons vary enormously. They measure quantities from ⅛ teaspoon to 1 tablespoon, necessary for such ingredients as baking powder, spices and salt, as well as some liquids. Unless a recipe says otherwise, all spoon measures are level – skim off the excess with a finger or the back of a knife.

OVEN THERMOMETER
Using the correct oven temperature is more essential for baking than for any other form of cooking. Ovens vary considerably and their reliability can falter, particularly as they get older. An oven thermometer sits or hangs on an oven shelf and will display the actual temperature, so you'll know whether to adjust your oven up or down. They're also good for working out where the hot and cooler spots are located so you can ensure your bakes cook evenly.

PASTRY BRUSHES AND PAINTBRUSHES
An indispensable yet inexpensive tool for **greasing** tins, brushing pastries with egg and for **glazes** after baking. Wooden-handled **pastry brushes** have a soft bristle that won't damage delicate pastry work, chocolate or fruit but they're not particularly heat-resistant and will wear quite quickly, particularly if you wash them in the dishwasher. Finer-bristled **paintbrushes** are useful for more delicate patisserie work, such as glazing thinner pastry edges.

PASTRY CUTTERS
A nest of **round pastry cutters** is useful for cutting out pastry bases and decorations and various sizes are used in this book. A double-sided set (plain on one side and

fluted on the other) gives you the choice of two finishes and means you don't need two separate sets cluttering up the cupboard. Metal cutters give the cleanest edge. Over time, you might want to build up a collection of more unusual cutter shapes.

PIPING BAGS AND NOZZLES

If you can, go for large, seamless, **nylon** piping bags: they have a little more strength to them, don't have seams for mixtures to leak through and are easy to wash after use. **Disposable plastic** piping bags in various sizes are available from most supermarkets or from specialist cake suppliers. The tip of a disposable or paper piping bag can be snipped off so you can pipe chocolate or icing in a thin line or random squiggles. Any other type of piping bag will need to be fitted with a piping nozzle. These also come in a range of sizes from wide tip ones for piping **choux pastry** and meringue, to tooth-edged ones for piping stars, and fine-tipped nozzles for writing and drizzling lines. Remember to fit the nozzle in the bag before adding the filling, as it's so easy to forget! Choose metal nozzles rather than plastic, as they'll last longer and pipe with more accuracy. Thoroughly wash and dry both nozzles and re-usable bags before storing and they'll last some time.

ROLLING PIN

Go for a fairly heavy wooden rolling pin with a diameter of about 6–7cm. Long rolling pins without handles are easy to grip and won't limit the width of the pastry that you can roll out.

RULER

Keep a ruler handy in the kitchen drawer for checking tin sizes and pastry thicknesses when rolling out. For some pastry and patisserie recipes you'll also need to cut rolled pastry accurately to a certain size. A washable ruler with metric and imperial measures is best.

SCALES

Wrongly weighed ingredients can lead to disaster so it pays to be accurate if you want perfect baking results every time. There are three types available, **spring, balance** (using weights) and **digital**. For ultra precision and convenience, digital scales are the best. They can measure ingredients as little as 1 gram and will switch between metric and imperial, solid and liquid measures. They'll also allow you to add and weigh several ingredients in the same bowl or pan simply by resting the vessel on the scales and resetting the scales to zero after adding each one. (Just remember to keep some spare batteries handy!)

SIEVE

Essential for removing lumps from icing sugar and flour if it's compacted during storage and for aerating flour as well as some puréeing tasks. Stainless steel is better than plastic as it's strong and durable and won't take on the colours and flavours of other ingredients. You'll get the most use out of one with a large bowl that sits easily over a mixing bowl. A small tea-strainer size is handy for dusting icing sugar and cocoa powder over pastry before serving.

SPATULA

A strong, flexible spatula is useful for mixing ingredients together, **folding in** and scraping out ingredients from mixing bowls so there's no wastage.

SUGAR THERMOMETER

Use a sugar thermometer to help you achieve the correct temperature when making caramel. Choose one that's not too big and cumbersome, and with a metal clip for securing it to one side of a pan. After use the thermometer is best left to soak in water (in the pan containing the leftover brittle caramel), where the caramel will dissolve away, rather than scraping at it and risking damage.

TIMER

Most ovens have an integral timer, but it's worth having another one handy in case you're leaving the kitchen while something's in the oven or you're timing a bake while you've also got something cooking on the hob, or even chilling. Go for one that has seconds as well as minutes, and with a long, loud ring. Set for a minute or two less than the suggested time in the recipe, especially if you are unsure of your oven temperature – you can always extend the cooking time if needed.

WHISKS AND MIXERS

These range from wire whisks that mean you have to do all the work, to free-standing mixers that do it all for you.

Wire whisks can be balloon-shaped or flat. A sturdy, hand-held wire whisk with an easy-grip handle that fits your hand is ideal for whisking, both on and off the heat.

Hand-held rotary whisks have two beaters in a metal frame, which are turned by hand. They're perfect for whisking egg whites and whisking mixtures over the heat, as there are no trailing electrical leads.

Hand-held electric whisks are more expensive, but very powerful, ideal for whisking cake mixtures, cream, egg whites and fillings.

Free-standing mixers are the most powerful and expensive of all, but save a lot of time and effort if you do plenty of baking. They have a large bowl and attachments for beating, whisking and kneading dough. If possible, buy an extra bowl too, as it helps when making cakes with multiple elements. Free-standing mixers do all the work for you, leaving you both hands free for getting on with other aspects of baking. To get the best from them, they're best left out on the work surface rather than away in a cupboard.

WOODEN SPOONS

Wooden spoons are heat-resistant and won't scratch the surface of your pans so they're ideal for mixing sauces, glazes and fillings over the hob, as well as for mixing cakes and icings. It's a good idea to keep a small selection of wooden spoons in various sizes, ideally keeping those used for savoury dishes separate as they can take on odours of other foods.

Skills

Once your ingredients are gathered and your equipment is at hand, you'll be ready to start baking. The recipes in this book take you stage by stage through all the skills and instructions you need, from the simpler bakes right through to the showstoppers at the end. As you work through the recipes, you'll find that some terms are written in bold, which means you can refer back to this section if you need clarification on a particular skill, or need to refresh your memory. There are also plenty of hints, tips and advice included to ensure that your bakes work brilliantly every time.

THE KEY PASTRY AND PATISSERIE TECHNIQUES

Because the sort of beautiful creations that you might find in a classic French patisserie can be so varied, you will find that you cover a wide range of baking skills as you work through the recipes in this book, but there are a few key techniques that will crop up time and again. Those key techniques are pastry, sponge cake and French meringue. This section will explain everything you need to know to achieve the best results from the main types of pastry used in this book: pâte sucrée (and pâte sablée), puff pastry, filo pastry and choux pastry, as well as how to achieve the perfect whisked sponge and French meringue. Some of the skills are very straightforward, others take a little more time, but all can be mastered with just a little patience.

PÂTE SUCRÉE (SWEET SHORTCRUST PASTRY)

This is a rich, buttery, sweet pastry that forms an integral part of traditional French patisserie, most commonly seen as the golden pastry case of many almond, fruit and custard tarts. Enriched with butter, sugar and egg yolks, it makes a firmer, crisper pastry than regular shortcrust, with a fuller, more biscuit-like flavour. It does however require more handling skills than shortcrust, as it can crack and collapse if it gets too warm. You might find it helpful to roll it out on a sheet of lightly floured baking paper – you can then move the paper, rather than the pastry, around as you roll. When you're ready to line your tin or tins, carefully turn the rolled-out pastry over the tin and peel away the paper. Then you can fit the pastry neatly into the tin.

1. Cream together the softened butter and sugar until soft and light in texture.

2. Mix in the egg yolks and flour with just a dash of water until the mixture starts to clump together (*see photo, right*).

3. Tip the dough out onto the work surface and **knead** just a few times until smooth, then shape it into a rough disc, wrap in clingfilm and **chill** for 30–45 minutes to firm up the butter and make it easier to roll out.

4. Roll out the pastry on a lightly floured surface to the thickness of a £1 coin (about 3mm), or the thickness stated in the recipe. In some patisserie recipes, very small tins are used, in which case the pastry needs to be rolled to just 2mm thickness. **Line** your tin or tins with it, easing the pastry into the corners with your fingertips. Chill for 15 minutes before baking.

Learn with: Frangipane Barquettes (page 76), French Apple Tart (page 102) and Chocolate Maple Tarts with Hazelnut Brittle (page 114)

PÂTE SABLÉE

Pâte sablée is similar to pâte sucrée and is used extensively in traditional French patisserie. Slightly richer and with a crisp snap due to its sweetness, pâte sablée is used both as a pastry case or base and for biscuits, a little like British shortbread. It's made in a similar way to pâte sucrée and is very much the same to work with.

Learn with: Salted Pecan Tartlets (page 70)

PUFF PASTRIES

Rough puff and puff pastries are similar in structure and flavour, but differ slightly in the way they are made. Both are richly flavoured with butter, where thin layers of air and fat are trapped between fine layers of dough to make a rising, flaky, layered treat. They're ideal for both sweet

and savoury pastries and feature greatly in patisserie classics such as Millefeuilles, Arlettes, Pithiviers and Palmiers.

You can use regular plain flour or strong white bread flour for both rough puff and puff pastry. Strong flour will give a flakier texture because the extra gluten it contains makes the dough stronger and more elastic, giving extra lift to the pastry to create the layers. The stronger structure also means the dough can withstand all the extra handling that puff pastry requires. Lemon juice helps the pastry keep its fresh colour throughout all the handling.

Both puff pastry and rough puff require a very hot oven for their layers to rise. They are deliciously buttery to eat but lose their crispness after a few hours. Reheating them can refresh the flavour and texture but it's best to eat the pastry on the day of baking. You can prepare the pastry the day before and chill overnight, wrapped in clingfilm or a polythene food bag, or freeze ahead.

Rough puff pastry

Rough puff is a sort of 'cheat's' puff pastry (see page 26). It uses the same combination of butter and flour but the butter is chopped into the dough rather than added in a single slab and the pastry is not rolled and folded as much. It doesn't puff up as much as 'proper' puff pastry, but it is flaky, buttery and delicious, making it a perfect substitute for puff pastry when you haven't got time to make the real thing. Rough puff pastry freezes well for 1–2 months. Defrost overnight in the fridge.

1. Add small cubes of very cold butter to flour and salt and stir together to coat.

2. Using a round-bladed knife, cut through the butter to make the pieces smaller, but still fairly lumpy (*see photo, left*).

3. Add cold water and lemon juice to form a fairly soft, rough-textured dough. Unlike smooth pastry dough, rough puff dough should look lumpy and slightly shaggy at this stage.

4. Shape your dough into a small rectangle, ready to roll out, then roll, fold and chill several times to create the flaky layers.

5. For the first rolling, roll out your dough on a well-floured surface with a well-floured rolling pin, to a rectangle about three times as long as its width with a short end facing you. The dough will look a bit streaky with butter, but the more it is rolled and folded, the smoother it'll become.

6. Fold the bottom third of the pastry up, then the top third down over the folded piece to make a three-layered rectangle (*see photo, right*).

7. Seal the edges by pressing with a rolling pin, give the dough a quarter turn clockwise, then press your rolling pin across the dough two or three times to hold the layers together a little.

8. Repeat the rolling, folding, sealing and turning.

9. Wrap the dough in clingfilm and chill in the freezer for 15 minutes to firm it up quickly.

10. Do two more rollings and foldings, including the sealing and turning. If any butter oozes out, use extra flour on the rolling pin and surface to stop it sticking. Your dough should now look smooth. Wrap and chill in the fridge for at least 1 hour or overnight before use. If you're short of time you can speed up the chilling by putting the pastry in the freezer for roughly half the time that it takes in the fridge.

Learn with: Palmiers with Gingerbread Spices (page 64) and Cranberry and Almond Eccles Cakes (page 80)

Puff pastry

Puff pastry has even more rich flaky layers than rough puff. You only mix in a very small amount of fat initially; most of the butter is added in one block later, then the dough is rolled and re-rolled to produce a pastry with even more layers, and more puff.

1. Rub in a small amount of the fat with the flour and salt.

2. Form a fairly soft dough with water and a little lemon juice.

3. Knead your dough on a lightly floured work surface for no more than a couple of minutes, just until you have a smooth dough, then put it in a bowl, cover with clingfilm and **chill** for 30 minutes.

4. Shape your butter into a small square and lay it between two sheets of baking paper, then use a rolling pin to press it into a square that's about 1cm thick (*see photo, top left*).

5. Shape your chilled dough into a square and **roll** it out on a lightly floured surface to the size stated in the recipe.

6. Peel off one sheet of paper from the butter and upturn the butter over the centre of the dough so the corners of the butter come halfway along (and slightly in from) the centre of the dough sides. Peel away the rest of the paper from the butter (*see photo, bottom left*).

7. Bring each corner of the dough up over the butter, so it's completely enclosed and you have a square envelope shape.

8. Make two or three indents across the dough with your rolling pin, which will also squash the butter a bit. Roll the dough out again using short, sharp movements and keeping the pastry as rectangular as possible.

9. Fold the bottom third up over the dough and the top third down over the folded dough to make a three-layered rectangle, then press the rolling pin firmly along the edges to seal the layers together. Give the dough a quarter turn clockwise. Push a hole in the dough (*see photo, right*) to remind you how many rolls and folds you've made.

10. Lightly flour the dough and place in a polythene food bag, keeping the edge you had in front of you on the work surface at the front in the fridge. Chill for 20 minutes.

11. Repeat as you did the second rolling, folding and turning, four more times. You don't need to chill it for the third and fifth rollings unless the dough becomes too sticky to handle. Each time you chill the dough, make little holes (two for the second rolling, four for the fourth etc) to remind you where you're up to. After the final rolling, wrap and chill for at least 2 hours before using.

Learn with: Cinnamon Arlettes with Blackberry Jelly (page 118) and Almond Pithiviers with Apricots (page 132)

FILO PASTRY

Filo pastry has characteristically paper-thin sheets of dough and is usually layered up and used to line baking tins or rolled up like a Swiss roll around a filling. Several recipes in this book use bought filo pastry, but making your own is not that difficult. The basic dough must be silky smooth and well rested before rolling, as it will have become very elastic during kneading. A dash of vinegar is added to help elasticity, though lemon juice can be used instead. The dough needs to be rolled out very thinly to achieve the characteristic flaky layers. Dusting with cornflour as you roll will help stop the sheets sticking together. The beauty of filo pastry is that it generally doesn't matter if there are creases and tears, as long as the layers are brushed well with melted butter.

Learn with: Cardamom and Orange Baklava (page 162)

CHOUX PASTRY

Choux pastry is unique in that it uses a large proportion of liquid to flour and an even larger proportion of egg, which produces its light, delicate texture, puffing up as it bakes to create an inner cavity – perfect for filling with delicious concoctions such as crème patissière. The most basic choux recipe is unsweetened and features widely in savoury recipes, but in this book, it's lightly sweetened to make classic patisserie dishes. Choux is not difficult to make but it's important to get the proportions of ingredients right and to follow the recipe accurately. It's a good idea to cut the butter into pieces to melt it before bringing to the boil otherwise the water will be boiling away before the butter is melted and the ratio of liquid will be inaccurate. The amount of egg beaten in also needs careful watching.

If you don't have time to bake choux pastry immediately, scrape it into a small bowl with a spatula, cover the surface with clingfilm to prevent a skin forming and chill for several hours or overnight before baking.

How to make choux pastry by hand
1. Sift the flour onto a square of baking paper so it's ready to tip quickly into the butter and water as soon as they're boiling.
2. Cut the butter into small pieces and put it in a medium pan. Add the sugar, salt and water and heat gently until the butter has melted. Increase the heat and cook until the liquid is at a rolling boil. Immediately tip in the flour, all in one go.
3. With the pan still on the heat, beat the ingredients with a wooden spoon. At first the flour will be lumpy but the mixture will smooth out as you beat it, eventually coming away from the sides of the pan as a thick ball of paste (*see photo, left*).

4. Tip the mixture into a large bowl and leave until the paste stops steaming. Beat the mixture several times as it cools – this will take about 3–4 minutes. Beating will speed up the cooling process and evaporate excess moisture, so that more egg can be beaten in, resulting in lighter, puffier pastry.
5. Start to beat in the beaten egg, a tablespoon at a time. Beat well with a wooden spoon to ensure that the egg is thoroughly absorbed before adding any more. At first it'll feel as if it's not being absorbed but it'll suddenly be taken up and become smoothly combined. At this stage, add more egg and beat well. It'll become easier to incorporate the egg as more is absorbed. Stop beating in the egg when the paste becomes glossy and quite smooth with a soft dropping consistency. This means it should fall easily from the spoon when lifted and not quite hold its shape when stirred. You might find that you don't need all the egg.
Learn with: Vanilla Chouquettes (page 90) and Passion Fruit Éclairs (page 92)

How to make choux pastry using a food-processor
1. Make the choux paste in a pan as above, to the end of step 3. Instead of tipping it into a bowl to cool, let it cool for a few minutes in the pan, beating frequently with a wooden spoon.
2. Tip the paste into a food-processor and add a tablespoon of the beaten egg. Blend briefly until the egg is absorbed. Continue to add the beaten egg, a little at a time until about half is blended in.
3. Scrape the mixture down from the sides of the bowl with a spatula and gradually add the remainder, stopping when the pastry has the consistency described in step 5 above.

WHISKED SPONGE
Whisked sponges rely on whisked eggs, rather than the addition of raising agents, to make them light and fluffy. It's a very versatile cake-making method, used extensively in patisserie recipes. Cake mixtures where whole eggs and sugar are whisked together are also known as 'génoise' sponges and may, or may not, have a small quantity of melted, cooled butter folded into the mixture right at the end, after the flour. This makes the sponge softer and richer.

'Biscuit' sponges are also whisked, but the yolks and whites are whisked separately with the sugar and combined later. These sponges are slightly drier and are often used for multi-layered creations as they are more robust.

Before you start, make sure that your eggs are at room temperature to aid expansion and that you have the melted butter ready and cooling before you start whisking. Ideally use a hand-held electric whisk or a large free-standing mixer fitted with a whisk attachment. If you only have a rotary or balloon whisk it helps if you rest the mixing bowl over a pan of steaming hot water (but don't let the bottom of the bowl touch the hot water). The gentle warmth increases the expansion of the eggs (be very careful!).

How to make a simple whisked sponge
1. **Whisk** the eggs and sugar at high speed for at least 5 minutes, until the colour changes from bright yellow to a very pale, creamy colour and the volume increases about five-fold. You should have a thick, mousse-like, foamy consistency. You can tell that the mixture is ready when it passes the 'ribbon test'. To do this lift the whisk out of the mixture – if a very distinct ribbon-like trail of mixture falls back into the bowl, you can stop whisking.

2. At this point, sift the flour into the bowl and gently **fold** into the foamy mixture (*see photo, top left*). This very light sponge is raised entirely by the air bubbles, so the folding in must be done with a light touch.

3. If melted butter is being added to the sponge, have this ready and cooled. If added while very hot it'll quickly fall to the base of the bowl and be harder to incorporate. Carefully drizzle it over the surface of the mixture rather than pouring it all into the centre, and fold in using a large metal spoon.
Learn with: Lemon Thyme Madeleines (page 68)

How to make a 'biscuit' sponge

1. Carefully separate the egg whites from the yolks and melt the butter.

2. Whisk the whites to **soft peaks**, then gradually whisk in half the sugar, a couple of teaspoons at a time, to make a light meringue.

3. Add the remaining caster sugar to the yolks and whisk until it is mousse-like and falls in thick ribbons from the whisk.

4. Fold a third of the meringue into the mousse mixture. This will help lighten the mixture so it's easier to fold in the remaining meringue mixture.

5. Sift the flour into the bowl and fold into the foamy mixture. This very light sponge is raised entirely by the air bubbles, so the folding in of the flour must be done with care and a light touch.

6. If melted butter is being added to the sponge, have this ready and cooled. If added while very hot it'll quickly fall to the base of the bowl and be harder to incorporate. Carefully drizzle it over the surface of the mixture and fold in using a large metal spoon (*see photo, bottom left*).
Learn with: Chocolate Pistachio Gateau (page 176)

FRENCH MERINGUE

This is the most frequently used method of making meringue. It can be made in a bowl with a hand-held electric mixer or in a free-standing mixer using the whisk attachment. Make sure that your bowl and whisk are completely clean and dry, as any grease or water will stop your egg whites from stiffening. The trick is to add the sugar at the right stage. The egg whites should be at soft peak stage; if you add the sugar too early it will dissolve and make the mixture soft and damp, but if the egg whites are too stiff the structure won't be elastic enough and will result in a lumpy meringue.

1. Put the egg whites in a large bowl and **whisk** until they form **soft peaks** (*see photo, top right*); do not over-whisk at this stage or the egg whites will turn to liquid again.

2. Add the sugar gradually, a spoonful at a time, and whisk well between each addition to ensure the sugar is fully whisked in before adding more, otherwise the meringue will have a grainy texture. Adding the sugar too quickly can also result in sugar syrup seeping out of the meringues during baking, which will spoil the finished appearance and crisp texture of the meringues.

3. Continue whisking until all the sugar is added and the meringue is firm, glossy and has reached the **stiff peak** stage (*see photo, bottom right*). The meringue is now ready to be piped or shaped and baked.

Learn with: Strawberry Rose Meringues (page 52) and Black Forest Meringues (page 78)

EXPERT ADVICE FROM START TO FINISH

This section takes you through the general techniques of making pastry and patisserie, from basic pastry methods to whisking egg whites and folding in.

USING BOUGHT PASTRY

Using bought pastry is a great way to get comfortable with handling pastry, and it's perfect for when time is short, particularly for recipes using puff pastry, which is more time-consuming to make from scratch. Most pastry is sold in either blocks that you roll yourself, or sheets that are rolled out and ready to use. Make sure frozen bought pastry is completely defrosted before using. If chilled, take it out of the fridge 10–15 minutes before use so that it's easier to handle.

Many of the recipes in this book use bought pastry, although you can, of course, make your own, following the instructions on these pages. Any excess pastry to the required amount freezes well in a polythene food bag. Collect the excess quantities until you have enough for a recipe. When saving up rough puff or puff pastry trimmings, stack the offcuts on top of one another, rather than rolling into a ball, so you keep all the layers.

Bought sweet shortcrust is a slightly sweetened type of shortcrust pastry, sold in blocks. It's good for making tart cases and makes a useful substitute for pâte sucrée when you're short of time.

Bought puff comes as puff and all-butter puff, available in a block or as a ready-rolled sheet. They can be used interchangeably, but all-butter puff tends to puff up more because of its higher fat content (plus it has a more buttery taste).

Bought filo packets contain a roll of readymade sheets. As this type of pastry is wafer thin, it can dry out very quickly, so have everything ready and your filling entirely cold before you take the pastry out of the packet. Carefully unroll it and work with one sheet at a time, immediately covering the other sheets with a clean tea towel or sheet of clingfilm, or they'll dry out and become too brittle. Store filo pastry in the fridge where it'll keep for up to 3 weeks (check the best-before date), then up to 3 days once the pack is opened. It can also be frozen for up to a month but the thin sheets are more likely to crack and sometimes stick to themselves after freezing and thawing.

As the sheets are so thin, you'll need to build up layers to provide enough thickness for your pastry. Brush a thin layer of oil or butter over each sheet. This helps give filo pastry its crispness and flaky layers. If you need to cut the pastry use a sharp knife so it doesn't tear. If it does tear when building up the layers, simply patch it up with more pastry. Filo pastry comes in a range of sizes, so you may need to adapt the layering or shaping according to the size you have, or use a different number of sheets than suggested in the recipe. You can also make your own (see page 27).

HOW TO RUB IN

The traditional way to make pastry is to use the rubbing-in technique. In this book, that applies to the first stage of making puff pastry or when making soured cream pastry or an enriched pastry (see Goats' Cheese and Olive Straws, page 50). In many traditional recipes both butter and lard are used to flavour pastry but in this book only butter is used for its richness and full flavour. Rubbing in refers to the way you combine the fat and flour through rubbing the fat into the flour using your fingertips (or a food-processor or mixer). It aerates your mixture, giving a lighter finish to your bake and ensuring that flour particles are well coated in fat before the water is added, which helps prevent the gluten from overdeveloping and becoming less 'short'. It's important to keep everything as cool as possible, including your hands and the water you use to combine the dough. After rubbing in you can then **form** a dough.

How to rub in by hand
1. Put your flour and any other dry ingredients in a large mixing bowl. There's no need to sift the flour as the process of rubbing in will remove any lumps and add air.
2. Take your butter straight from the fridge and cut into dice. Tip into the flour and stir it around with a round-bladed knife so each piece is coated.
3. Pick up a little of the butter and flour mixture with your fingers. Slide your thumbs across your fingertips so the butter breaks down into even smaller pieces and starts to combine with the flour to make finer crumbs that fall back into the bowl (*see photo*).
4. Repeat, lifting your hands well above the bowl so the mixture can fall back into it from a height, to aerate it further, until the mixture looks like breadcrumbs. The coarseness of the breadcrumb stage will depend on the ratio of butter to flour – when making puff pastry only a small amount of butter is used initially so the mixture will still look very floury.

How to rub in using a food-processor
1. Put your flour and chilled, diced butter (plus any other dry ingredients such as salt) in the food-processor.

2. Pulse in short, sharp bursts until it looks like breadcrumbs have been formed. This should only take a few seconds. Stop as soon as you get to this stage otherwise the mixture will be overworked and stick together before you add further ingredients.

HOW TO FORM A DOUGH

Different types of dough require different ingredients to bind them together, like water, egg yolks, soured cream and cheese. Some doughs should be quite soft, such as rough puff and puff, while pâte sucrée needs to be firmer. Bear in mind that cooked pastry will have a better texture and consistency if it's not over-handled when you form the dough.

How to form a dough by hand

1. After rubbing in, add the egg yolk or yolks, water or other ingredients such as soured cream.

2. Stir with a round-bladed knife until it starts to clump together. At this stage, take over with your hands, as it's much easier to gauge consistency with your hands. Start gathering the ingredients into one big ball. If there are lots of dry bits in the bottom of the bowl, add a teaspoon or so of water to help work them into the dough.

3. Run the dough around the edges of the bowl to pick up stray pieces and turn out onto the surface ready for kneading and shaping.

How to form a dough using a food-processor

1. Add the liquid, plus any other ingredients and pulse again, keeping an eye out for the moment it starts to clump together, then switch off the machine.

2. Remove the lid and pinch some of the mixture between your fingers – if it doesn't stick together easily or it feels a little dry, add a drop more water and pulse again, but don't over-process as this will toughen the dough and stretch it, causing shrinkage later on.

3. Tip your dough out onto a lightly floured surface and gently gather into a ball.

HOW TO KNEAD AND SHAPE DOUGH

Put your ball of dough on a lightly floured surface and bring it gently together with your hands, folding it over to knead it only a few times, just enough to achieve a smooth consistency. Don't knead as you would for bread, you just want to get the dough to come smoothly together. Puff pastry should be kneaded only very briefly, to avoid the gluten developing too much. Flatten it slightly into the shape you want to end up with after rolling it out (circle, square or rectangle) to make it easier to keep that shape as you roll it. Wrap it in clingfilm and **chill** (see below) to firm up.

HOW TO CHILL PASTRY

All of your pastries, except choux, will benefit from being chilled and rested. Chilling firms up the fat, which makes pastry easier to roll out and reduces the risk of shrinkage when cooking. It also 'relaxes' the dough so that it doesn't keep shrinking back after each roll. This is particularly important with puff and rough puff as they become very elastic with the repeated rolling and folding. The pastry doughs in this book benefit from at least 20–30 minutes chilling. Those rich in butter require longer, about 1 hour, to firm up. You can speed up chilling by freezing the dough for about half the time you'd chill it in the fridge. Pastry can also be chilled overnight but you might need to let it sit at room temperature for 10–15 minutes before rolling, as it will have become very firm.

HOW TO ROLL OUT PASTRY

The key to rolling out pastry is to use as little flour as you need to prevent the pastry sticking to the surface and rolling pin. Dust both lightly before you start and don't put flour directly on the pastry. If you use too much flour the dough will become dry and crumbly.

When rolling puff and rough puff you'll need more flour than you would for other pastries because of the quantity of butter within the dough. A rich pastry like pâte sucrée can start to crack as you roll it out (because of the extra fat content); if this happens, try laying a large sheet of lightly floured baking paper on the work surface and rolling out the pastry on top – you can then move the paper around on the work surface as you roll, rather than the pastry.

1. Start by flattening out the dough a bit more with your rolling pin.
2. Move the dough around on the surface so it's lightly coated in the flour, then start to roll it out in short, sharp movements, working from the edge nearest you and rolling the dough away from you. Don't turn the dough over.
3. After a few rolls, give the dough a quarter turn and roll again. As you keep doing this the dough will get thinner and you can check that it's not sticking to the surface by frequently giving it a quarter turn. You might need to move it to one side while you sprinkle a tiny bit more flour on the surface.
4. As you roll, keep the dough to the desired shape as best you can. For lining a round tin you can roll the dough in all directions

to achieve a round shape but if you want to end up with a square shape (for lining a square tin or cutting into smaller squares or rectangles), always roll the pastry up and down or across so you keep the edges as straight as possible.

5. As the pastry gets thinner, check that you're rolling it to the right size. The recipe will state either the thickness required or the dimensions to roll out to. You might need a ruler handy. For pâte sucrée, pate sablée and other pastries for lining tins, the thickness is usually 2–3mm (about the thickness of a £1 coin). Aim to get your pastry this fine as it'll give a crisper crust and more professional, tastier result. Puff and rough puff, Danish pastries and croissants are often rolled thicker as the pastry needs to rise and puff up into layers as it bakes.

HOW TO CUT OUT YOUR PASTRY

When cutting rectangles or squares of pastry, or using pastry cutters to line small tart tins, aim to create as clean a cut edge as possible. If you are cutting freehand, such as creating even-sized squares for the Danish Pastries on page 142, use a large, sharp knife and if it starts to stick, dip it in a little flour.

When using cutters it is important to try and get as many shapes as you can from the first rolling (as it will have been handled less). Sit your cutter on the edge of the pastry, then firmly and evenly press it down with the palm of your hand in one movement. If you move it around you may distort the shape. Lift the cutter off and lift the pastry shape up with a small palette knife. For the next shape, position the cutter as close to the last cut-out shape as possible. It can really help to dip your pastry cutter in flour first, to stop it sticking.

HOW TO LINE A TIN WITH PASTRY

Whatever you're lining, your pastry needs to fit snugly in the tin, with no air pockets, creases, folds or cracks that will affect the finished result.

To line a large tart tin

1. Roll out your pastry to the correct size. Drape it over your rolling pin, lift it up and carefully lower it into the tin, checking that it's evenly centred.

2. Once it's roughly in position, lower it further into the tin, bit by bit, so you can ease it into the corners and make sure there are no air pockets on the bottom. Work your way around the tin, pushing and smoothing the pastry onto the base and then into the sides and flutes (if there are any), keeping it even thickness. Once you've worked all around the sides of the case, let the excess pastry hang over the edges, ready for trimming.

3. The easiest way to trim away the excess pastry is to roll your rolling pin over the top of the tin – the sharp edges of the tin will cut off the overhanging pastry. When you've finished, press the pastry around the sides of the tin again so it extends slightly above the rim.

4. If any cracks have developed while lining the tin, try and eliminate them now. This sometimes happens with pâte sucrée and is easy to rectify by pushing a little of the pastry trimmings into the crack and moulding it, like putty, until it smooths out.

To line tartlet tins

1. Roll out the pastry as above to 2mm thickness.

2. Take one of your tartlet tins and rest it over the pastry. Cut the pastry out around the tin so the dimensions of the pastry are about 4cm larger than the size of the tin. For round tins, it's easier to cut around a small bowl or saucer once you know what size you're cutting. Use the cut-out shapes to line the tins, easing the pastry into the corners and up the sides (*see photo on page 37, top*). Trim off the excess pastry around the tops with a small sharp knife. Gather up the trimmings and re-roll them so that you have enough pastry to line all the tins.

HOW TO BLIND BAKE

Tarts with softer fillings use this technique where the pastry case is baked first, while the tart is empty. It helps prevent the pastry becoming soggy on the bottom.

1. After lining your tin, prick the pastry base lightly with a fork. (Don't push the fork all the way through the pastry or the holes might cause the filling to leak). **Chill** the pastry in its tin.

2. While chilling, preheat the oven and place a baking sheet in the oven to heat up, ready for cooking the tart.

3. Lay a piece of baking paper over the pastry so it's large enough to line the base and extend up the sides of the tin.

4. Tip in some baking beans or uncooked rice to form a thickish layer (about 1.5–2cm deep, depending on the depth of your tin) to hold the pastry down. Spread the beans in an even layer, making sure the beans and paper fit right up against the sides of the tin so the pastry is supported (*see photo on page 37, bottom*).

5. Part-bake the pastry on the baking sheet to firm it up and set it into shape. At this stage the pastry will still be pale and not yet browning. The important thing is that the pastry is now firm enough that the sides won't collapse when you remove the paper and beans.

6. Lift out the paper and beans (carefully as

the beans will be very hot) and return the pastry case to the oven, still on the baking sheet, to finish cooking. The base and sides should be pale golden and cooked through, ready for filling.

HOW TO PATCH UP PASTRY CRACKS

Cracks can sometimes appear after blind baking, usually if you are using a richer pastry like pâte sucrée, so it's a good idea to keep any scraps of uncooked pastry wrapped and handy just in case. Check your pastry case after the first bake; to fill a crack, take a very small piece of uncooked pastry and smooth it gently and evenly over the crack. Don't overfill the crack or you'll make the pastry base or sides too thick.

HOW TO GLAZE

There are several ways of glazing pastry and patisserie to add flavour and/or make them more visually appealing.

Beaten egg glazes, applied to pastries before baking, give a golden colour and are also used to secure one piece of pastry to another, such as decorative leaves. Some recipes use a whole beaten egg, while others use just the yolk, thinned with a little water. The egg yolk gives a richer, glossier glaze that gives instant colour – useful when the pastry is fast baked.

Occasionally sugar is sprinkled over the egg glaze before baking to give a crunchier texture. Demerara sugar is particularly good for this. In the case of the Almond Pithiviers with Apricots (see page 132), a snow-like dusting of icing sugar is sprinkled over the baked pastry, then returned to an extremely hot oven where the sugar caramelises to a glossy, rich sheen that looks highly professional.

Fruit glazes are made from jam, jelly and marmalade and add flavour and shine after baking. To make them thin enough to brush on, melt them first or add a little boiling water to thin. If using a jam with bits of fruit in it you might prefer to press it through a sieve so your glaze is ultra smooth.

HOW TO GREASE AND LINE TINS

Some pastry and patisserie recipes require you to line, grease, or grease and line a tin or baking sheet before you start. Baking sheets are easy enough to line with a sheet of baking paper (or re-usable liner) for easy removal of your pastries. When you need to grease a tin for a recipe, use a little extra melted butter and brush it with a pastry brush in a thin film. If the tin then needs lining, you can do this by placing the tin on the baking paper and cutting around it (to line the base), and then cutting further strips for the sides, if necessary. Occasionally a recipe requires a tin or mould to be 'greased and floured'. This is usually for shaped tins such as ring moulds where it would be difficult to line it with paper. Brush the tin or mould with melted butter then sprinkle in a little flour. Keep tilting and turning the tin so that the flour coats the entire surface (*see photo, left*). Tap out the excess flour so there are no areas that are thickly coated.

HOW TO WHISK EGG WHITES

Egg whites need a large, spotlessly clean and grease-free bowl. Any trace of fat stuck to the bowl or egg yolk that's got into it, or onto the whisk, will prevent the whites from being beaten successfully – you can cut a lemon in half and run the cut side around the inside of the bowl and over the whisk to be really sure. Use egg whites at room temperature for best results and don't stop midway through beating as this can break down the meringue, which will lose volume.

1. Put the egg whites in the bowl and whisk on a low speed (or slowly by hand) for about 30 seconds so they become frothy and the structure starts to develop.

2. Add a pinch of cream of tartar or a drop of lemon juice at this point, as the slight acidity will help the structure to stiffen so you achieve the maximum volume.

3. Increase the speed and continue whisking until the mixture is a mass of tiny bubbles with a very smooth and fine texture. To tell if the whites have reached **soft peak** stage, lift the whisk out of the mixture – you should get a peak of egg white that slightly droops down (*see photo on page 31, top*). If you are making meringues, add the sugar at this stage (see page 31).

4. If you continue whisking, you will get to the **stiff peak** stage – when you take the whisk out the peak will stand upright with no droop. You should also be able to turn the bowl upside down without the whites falling out (see the photo on page 31, bottom).

....

HOW TO FOLD IN
This is the way to delicately combine two or more ingredients – for example adding sifted flour to a whisked sponge, folding meringue into a nut paste for macarons (see page 106), or into a chocolate mousse. The gentle touch is required so that you don't beat out all the air you've carefully beaten in. Use the edge of a large metal spoon or plastic spatula to cut down cleanly through the centre of the mixture until you touch the bottom of the bowl, then turn the spoon the right way up and bring it up through the mixture to the top. Turn the spoon over so the contents flop

gently onto the rest of the mixture. Give the bowl a quarter turn so that you start from a different place, then cut down again through the mixture, lift it and flop it over again. Keep doing this folding action, using the least number of movements possible, until you can't see any streaks.

....

HOW TO WHIP CREAM
Cream should be thoroughly chilled before whipping. If it's not – particularly in warm weather – it's more likely to curdle. Double cream is used when you need more body, whereas whipping cream is lighter and airier. Use a hand-held wire whisk, hand-held rotary whisk, electric whisk or free-standing mixer. Whisk on a medium speed to a **soft peak**, slowing down as the cream thickens so you can better gauge when it's ready. When the cream reaches a soft peak that flops over slightly it's ready for folding in or for other uses. Whisking for a few more seconds will take the cream to **stiff peak** stage, although do take care not to over-whip cream as its consistency is quickly spoilt. If you are going to pipe the cream, take it to almost stiff-peak stage – but be careful not to over-whip the cream as it will continue to thicken as you pipe it.

....

HOW TO PIPE
Cream, meringue, choux pastry, sponge mixtures and crème patissière are just some of the ingredients used for piping, but the process of filling a piping bag and piping is roughly the same.

....

How to fill a piping bag
First fit the piping bag with the required nozzle, dropping it into the end and positioning it so it fits snugly at the end of the bag. Twist the bag right above the

nozzle so the mixture doesn't ooze out while you're filling it. Put the bag in a tall glass and fold the top of the bag over the rim. (The glass will support the bag so it's easier to fill.) Spoon the mixture into the bag until about two-thirds full (*see photo, left*). Unfold the bag from the rim and twist the top to push the mixture down to the piping end, eliminating any air bubbles. Untwist the nozzle end and squeeze the bag so that the mixture fills the nozzle.

How to pipe
A firm and steady hand is essential to ensure smooth and even piping, so hold the piping bag in both hands with your stronger hand at the top of the bag and your other hand at the bottom near the nozzle to help guide the bag. Squeeze the bag gently, using even pressure so that the mixture comes out in a smooth flow. If you are piping rounds such as the French Macarons with Raspberries (page 106), draw circles on the baking paper and then flip it over so you can see the pencil lines to achieve consistent sizes.

HOW TO MAKE SUGAR SYRUP AND CARAMEL

Sugar syrup is made by dissolving sugar in water. By boiling the syrup it becomes thicker and then eventually turns golden, making a caramel. The key to success is to make sure that the sugar has completely dissolved and the liquid is clear before starting to boil it. Overheating the syrup can also cause crystallisation where small hard, white crystals form. White sugar is generally used, as it's easier to gauge when it starts to colour, though with experience it's possible to make syrups and caramels with brown sugars for a fuller flavour. Use a small, clean heavy-based pan and have everything ready to use once the caramel reaches the right temperature as it sets brittle very quickly. It's also worth having a bowl half filled with cold water so you can dip the base of the pan in it, to prevent further cooking. Take care not to overcook the caramel as it will develop a bitter flavour and burn.

How to make sugar syrup
1. Put the required amount of sugar and water in a small pan and heat very gently until the sugar dissolves. Don't stir the mixture; just let it heat very gently until the liquid starts to clear. Only draw a spoon through if there's a concentrated area of sugar.
2. Use a wet pastry brush to wash down the sides of the pan and prevent any sugar crystals forming (*see photo, right*).
3. Once the liquid is completely clear, increase the temperature so the sugar starts to boil and thicken slightly.

How to make caramel
1. Follow steps 1–3 above. Clip a sugar thermometer to the pan, if using. Continue to boil the syrup for 5–10 minutes, at which point it will start to turn golden. Watch closely as it will colour quickly.
2. For making nut brittle, praline and spun sugar, continue to cook the caramel until it turns to a golden, pale amber colour (or 155°C/310°F on the sugar thermometer). Very briefly (for just a few seconds) dip the base of the pan in cold water to stop the caramel browning further. Don't leave it so long that it starts to thicken before you've had a chance to use it.

Help!

No matter how experienced we are in the kitchen, for one reason or another, things just occasionally go wrong. Knowing what went wrong and why can help prevent the same situation happening again. Here are some of the more common problems you might come across and how you might solve them, or at least know how to prevent them next time.

WHY IS THE BOTTOM OF MY PASTRY CASE SOGGY?

Make sure you put a baking sheet in the oven when you switch it on ready for baking – putting your tart on a hot sheet starts the pastry cooking immediately to make it deliciously crisp. Most tarts are blind baked before filling; after blind baking the pastry base should be a good golden colour, so you may need to blind bake for a little longer. Your filling also may have been too warm when it went into the case, which can sometime melt the butter in the pastry. Also, pastry that hasn't been rolled thinly enough will take longer to cook through.

WHY IS MY PASTRY TOUGH?

The most likely reason is that too much water has been added or that you've overworked the pastry – handling it too much develops the gluten and creates a tough texture. Keep a light touch when kneading and shaping the dough next time.

MY PUFF PASTRY HASN'T PUFFED UP!

Puff pastry uses a lot of butter, which needs to stay very chilled during the whole process. If the butter softens, the pastry will be trickier to work with and the butter will seep out from the layers you're trying to build up. If at any stage the butter gets too soft, chill the dough by popping it in the freezer for 10–20 minutes before re-rolling.

It could also be that when you glazed your puff pastry with beaten egg, a little bit ran down the cut edge of the pastry, glueing the layers together instead of allowing them to puff in the heat of the oven.

Make sure your oven is hot enough, too, before baking the pastry, as it needs the high temperature to make the layers puff up. However, if the layers haven't puffed up as much as you wanted, the pastry will still be deliciously rich and buttery.

WHY IS MY CHOUX PASTRY TOUGH AND RUBBERY?

The large quantity of egg that is beaten into the choux pastry paste is what makes it rise up into the light billowy puffs that we love. Make sure the paste that you've beaten in the pan is really thick, making a ball of paste that comes away from the sides of the pan completely, before you start adding the beaten egg, so that you can incorporate the amount of egg required before it loses its shape. It could also be that you added the eggs before the paste had cooled properly, causing them to start 'cooking' in the heat of the paste. Unfortunately, if your baked choux pastry is tough, there's not a lot you can do to fix it.

WHY DID MY CAKE SINK IN THE MIDDLE?

This is probably because the cake wasn't baked long enough, or it was baked at the wrong temperature. Cakes require a really accurate oven temperature for success so you might want to check your oven's thermostat by using an oven thermometer. If the centre of the cake mixture doesn't get hot enough (around 100°C/212°F), then the structure won't become set and firm, and the middle of the cake will collapse as it cools. Use a kitchen timer and test for doneness before removing from the oven to cool: gently press the top of the sponge in the centre with your fingertips – the sponge is ready if it springs back into place and has started to shrink back from the sides of the tin. If a slight dent remains in the sponge after you press it (or it starts to sink), then leave it in the oven for a few more minutes. It's also important not to keep opening the oven door during baking. The blast of cold air is likely to collapse the delicate rising of the cake. If this happens, disguise the dip by filling it with fruit or whipped cream, or cut the cake into little pieces to serve.

THE SUGAR IS SEEPING OUT OF MY COOKED MERINGUES!

This is usually because the sugar has been added too quickly to the whisked egg whites. Once you've got the egg whites to the soft peaks stage, add just a tablespoon of the measured sugar and whisk again for about 15 seconds before you add another spoonful of the sugar. Continue to add the sugar a little at a time so each spoonful is thoroughly absorbed by the egg whites before adding any more. By doing this your meringue will end up thick and glossy, perfect for piping or spooning.

If your failed meringues don't look appetising enough to serve, break them into pieces and mix with chopped strawberries and lightly sweetened cream for an impromptu Eton Mess!

WHY ARE MY TARTS OVERFLOWING?

It's so tempting to squeeze in a little extra deliciously sweet or fruity filling into a tart, tartlet or pastry parcel. The problem is that the sugar in the filling will heat up into a boiling syrup and do its best to seep out, either onto the baking sheet or into the tart/tartlet cases or bun tin, where it'll stick firmly and stop you lifting the pastries out without spoiling them further. It's best to follow the quantities suggested and in the case of tarts and tartlets, leave a clear rim of pastry visible, even if you've a little bit of filling left.

An over-filled tart is usually fine to serve, even if it has stuck to your baking sheet. Run a palette knife around to release it – it may not look pristine but it will usually still taste good.

MY PASTRY IS READY BUT THE FILLING HASN'T COOKED YET!

This is an easy problem to remedy. If some areas or all of the pastry is nicely golden and you don't want to spoil it by cooking it any further, simply cover the pastry with foil. Tear strips of foil and cover the pastry edges, crumpling the foil around the edges of the tin. Watch closely as you put the tart back in the oven to check that the foil hasn't moved.

MY CREAM IS TOO STIFF!

This is an easy mistake to make when whipping cream: one minute it's soft and fluffy, the next it's standing in stiff peaks. The way to avoid this is to watch it very carefully and at the point when it starts to thicken, start to whisk more slowly in short, sharp bursts and keep checking the consistency regularly. If it does become too thick, pour in a little un-whipped cream and lightly fold through to loosen.

BAKE IT BETTER
Recipes

Chocolate Caramel Puffs

These delicious little pastries are a good practice bake before tackling advanced 'Viennoiserie' recipes. Using **bought puff pastry** makes them quick and easy too.

100g good-quality dark chocolate, preferably a minimum of 70 per cent cocoa solids
¼ teaspoon ground cinnamon
15g caster sugar
500g bought puff pastry block
5 teaspoons ready-made caramel sauce
1 egg yolk, to glaze

1. Preheat the oven to 190°C (170°C fan), 375°F, Gas 5 and **line** a baking sheet with baking paper.

2. Cut or break the chocolate into 10 even-sized portions. Mix together the cinnamon and sugar in a small bowl.

3. **Roll** out the **bought puff pastry** on a lightly floured surface to a 55 x 30cm rectangle. It's easier to keep the sides of the pastry straight if you always roll up and down, or across the dough rather than diagonally. Cut the pastry in half lengthways then make 4 evenly spaced cuts widthways so that you end up with 10 rectangles, each measuring about 15 x 11cm. Beat the egg yolk with ½ teaspoon cold water and use some of it to lightly brush the edges of the rectangles.

4. Spread ½ teaspoon of the caramel sauce into the centre of each rectangle, keeping it away from the edges. Position the chocolate pieces in the centre of each rectangle. For each pastry, bring one short end of the pastry up over the filling to cover it then bring the other short end up and over to cover that. Pinch the cut edge that runs down the length of the pastry together with the pastry underneath using your thumb and forefinger to seal them together. Then press the open ends firmly. Invert onto the baking sheet so the join is underneath and repeat with the remainder.

5. Brush with more egg yolk to **glaze** and bake for about 25 minutes or until puffed and golden. Immediately sprinkle with the cinnamon sugar and leave to cool slightly before eating.

Try Something Different

For a slightly sweeter flavour use white or milk chocolate instead of the dark.

HANDS-ON TIME:
15 minutes

BAKING TIME:
25 minutes

MAKES:
10 pastries

SPECIAL EQUIPMENT:
large baking sheet

PASTRY USED:
Bought puff, page 32

STORAGE:
Best eaten the same day while still slightly warm, or the next day, warmed through in a moderate oven for 5 minutes

Apple and Blackberry Turnovers

These flaky, fruity puffs make a great bake using **bought puff pastry**. The sweet, juicy filling is likely to burst out a little as the pastries cook in the oven, but this will only add to their lovely home-made appearance.

I large tart dessert apple, e.g. Cox's
½ teaspoon lemon juice
I teaspoon cornflour
I x 320g sheet bought puff pastry
75g blackberries
30g demerara sugar
I egg yolk, to glaze

HANDS-ON TIME:
25 minutes

BAKING TIME:
25 minutes

MAKES:
6 turnovers

SPECIAL EQUIPMENT:
large baking sheet

PASTRY USED:
Bought puff, page 32

STORAGE:
Best eaten the same day or the next day, warmed through in a moderate oven for 5 minutes

1. Preheat the oven to 190°C (170°C fan), 375°F, Gas 5 and **line** a baking sheet with baking paper. Peel, core and dice the apple. Make sure the pieces are no more than about 1cm in diameter so they'll fit easily inside the pastry parcels. Mix in a bowl with the lemon juice, then the cornflour.

2. Unroll the bought puff pastry sheet on its paper. Using a sharp knife cut the pastry in half lengthways then across into squares so you end up with six 11–12cm squares. Beat the egg yolk with ½ teaspoon cold water and use to lightly brush the edges of the squares.

3. Spoon the apples diagonally across the squares and place the blackberries on top. Make sure that each square contains about the same amount of fruit. Reserve 2 teaspoons of the sugar and sprinkle the rest over the fruit. Fold one corner of a pastry square over the filling and press down firmly onto the opposite corner. Press the pastry down firmly where the edges meet. Don't worry about being too heavy-handed with this as you need to make sure the pastry edges are sealed firmly together. Press the tines of a fork around the edges to further seal the pastry together.

4. Transfer to the baking sheet and brush with the remaining egg yolk to **glaze**. Score the tops with the tip of a knife so you can just see the filling inside. Sprinkle with the reserved sugar.

5. Bake for about 25 minutes until crisp and golden. Leave to cool on the baking sheet for at least 10 minutes before serving so the filling is not piping hot.

Try Something Different

For an autumn or winter bake, add a little spiciness to the fruits by sprinkling over a pinch of ground ginger or cinnamon with the sugar.

Goats' Cheese and Olive Straws

In this recipe black olives and mature goats' cheese give classic cheese straws a modern twist. The 'rub in' technique is used here, an essential skill for pastry cooks.

100g plain flour
80g chilled unsalted butter, diced
100g hard goats' cheese, finely grated
40g pitted black olives, finely chopped
1 teaspoon finely chopped oregano
1 medium egg yolk
sprigs of oregano, to scatter

1. Preheat the oven to 190°C (170°C fan), 375°F, Gas 5 and **line** a baking sheet with baking paper.

2. Put the flour in a medium bowl and add the butter. You won't need to add any salt to this recipe as the cheese and olives are salty enough. **Rub in** until the mixture looks like coarse breadcrumbs. Stir in the cheese, olives and chopped oregano until evenly distributed. Add the egg yolk and 1 teaspoon cold water and stir with a round-bladed knife until the mixture starts to clump together. Use your hands to compact the mixture into a ball of dough. (Alternatively make the pastry in a **food-processor**.) **Shape** into a flat block of dough, ready for rolling.

3. **Roll** out on a lightly floured surface to a 22cm square. Try and keep the sides of the pastry as square as you can by rolling up and down the dough, or across, rather than diagonally. Trim off the edges with a knife to neaten. Using a large sharp knife cut the dough in half. Transfer the two rectangles of dough onto the baking sheet then cut each piece widthways into 1cm-wide sticks. If the knife starts to stick, clean it and dip in a little flour. Nudge the sticks apart slightly with the side of the knife.

4. Bake for 17–20 minutes until pale golden. The cheese might bubble up during baking but will firm up on cooling. Leave on the baking sheet for a couple of minutes then transfer to a wire rack to cool completely. This is easiest done by scooping them up with a fish slice. Serve scattered with oregano sprigs.

Easy does it

HANDS-ON TIME:
20 minutes

BAKING TIME:
17–20 minutes

MAKES:
about 35 straws

SPECIAL EQUIPMENT:
large baking sheet

STORAGE:
Keep for up to 3 days in an airtight container

Try Something Different

Use a firm blue cheese such as Stilton instead of the goats' cheese and swap the oregano for ¾ teaspoon celery seeds.

Strawberry Rose Meringues

A hint of rose extract and fresh strawberries give these simple **French meringues** a delicate yet distinctive flavour, perfect for a stylish afternoon tea.

For the meringues
3 medium egg whites, at room temperature
pinch of salt
¼ teaspoon cream of tartar
175g caster sugar

For the topping
150ml whipping cream, well chilled
1 tablespoon icing sugar
½ teaspoon rose extract
12 medium strawberries
sprigs of mint (optional)

HANDS-ON TIME:
25 minutes, plus cooling

BAKING TIME:
50–60 minutes

MAKES:
12 meringues

SPECIAL EQUIPMENT:
2 baking sheets, large piping bag, star nozzle

METHOD USED:
French meringue, page 31

STORAGE:
The meringues keep for up to 5 days in an airtight container. Serve within several hours of decorating with cream and strawberries

1. Preheat the oven to 120°C (100°C fan), 250°F, Gas ½ and **line** two baking sheets with baking paper.

2. To make the meringue, put the egg whites, salt and cream of tartar into a large, spotlessly clean bowl. Gently **whisk** using a hand-held electric whisk to break up the egg whites. Increase the speed and whisk until the mixture stands in **soft peaks** when the whisk is lifted from the bowl. Add a rounded tablespoon of the sugar and whisk for a further 15 seconds. Add another spoonful of the sugar and whisk again. Continue to whisk in the sugar, a tablespoon at a time, and whisking well between each addition until the meringue is thick and glossy.

3. Using a dessertspoon, place a mound of the meringue on the baking paper. Add 5 more mounds of meringue to one baking sheet and 6 to the other, spacing them well apart. Press down with the back of the spoon to flatten slightly. Neaten the meringue into drum shapes by running a small palette knife vertically around the sides. The tops needn't be smoothed down as they'll be covered with cream. Bake for 50–60 minutes until the meringues feel crisp and dry. Leave to cool on the paper.

4. To make the topping, put the cream, icing sugar and rose extract in a medium bowl and **whip** with a hand-held electric whisk on a low speed until the cream only just forms soft peaks when the whisk is lifted from the bowl.

5. Lift the cooled meringues off the paper (they should come away very easily) and onto a serving plate or stand. Put the cream in a large piping bag fitted with a large star nozzle. **Pipe** the cream around the edges of the meringues, working in a spiral to the centre. Hull the strawberries, reserving some of the green parts for decoration if they are pretty. Thinly slice each strawberry and arrange in a fan shape over the cream, allowing one strawberry per meringue. Position the green parts, if using, or mint, in the centres to decorate.

Try Something Different

For a flavour alternative, omit the rose extract from the meringues and decorate with thin slices of mango or kiwi fruit. Top with a few fresh mint leaves.

Spinach and Ricotta Strudel

Using **bought filo pastry** is a great way to practise handling the delicate sheets of pastry before you tackle making your own filo (see page 27). The pastry layers are brushed with melted butter so they stay separate and crisp up beautifully as they bake.

50g pine nuts
50g unsalted butter
2 onions, finely chopped
2 garlic cloves, crushed
1 teaspoon ground coriander
1 teaspoon freshly ground black pepper

300g baby spinach leaves
250g ricotta
3 tablespoons double cream
6 sheets bought filo pastry, each about 46 x 25cm
salt

Easy does it

HANDS-ON TIME:
30 minutes, plus cooling

BAKING TIME:
30 minutes

SERVES:
6

SPECIAL EQUIPMENT:
baking sheet

PASTRY USED:
Bought filo, page 32

STORAGE:
Best served freshly baked, warm or cold

1. Dry-fry the pine nuts in a frying pan over a medium heat for 3–4 minutes, shaking the pan frequently, until the nuts are lightly toasted. Tip the nuts out onto a plate. Melt 15g of the butter in the pan, add the onions and fry gently for 3 minutes, stirring until softened. Add the garlic, coriander and pepper and cook, stirring for 1 minute. Stir in the spinach, turning it for 1 minute until it starts to wilt. Turn off the heat but keep turning the spinach in the pan until it has wilted evenly but not completely collapsed. Leave to cool.

2. Drain off any liquid from the surface of the ricotta. Put the ricotta in a bowl. Stir in the cream and a little salt. Melt the remaining butter in a small pan.

3. Preheat the oven to 190°C (170°C fan), 375°F, Gas 5. **Line** a baking sheet with baking paper. Unroll the 6 filo sheets. Spread one sheet out on the work surface. Lay another sheet next to it, along its long edge, overlapping the two sheets by 5cm. Brush all over with a little melted butter. Place two more overlapping sheets on top,

this time with the overlapping edges going in the opposite direction. Brush the second layer lightly with butter. Distribute the spinach mixture over the pastry, leaving an 8cm border all around. Dot the ricotta mixture on top and spread it roughly to cover. Reserve 1 tablespoon of the pine nuts and scatter the remainder over the ricotta. Season with a little salt.

4. Fold two opposite edges of pastry about 2cm over the filling so it doesn't leak out. From an unfolded edge, roll up the strudel loosely. Transfer to the baking sheet (use a fish slice to support one end as you move it). Brush with more melted butter.

5. Take another sheet of filo pastry and lay it over the log, scrunching it up into pleats and tucking the ends under the strudel. Brush with more butter and scrunch the remaining filo sheet on top. Brush with the rest of the butter and scatter with the reserved pine nuts. Bake for 30 minutes until the pastry is crisp and golden. This is lovely served warm or cold with a leafy salad.

Poppy Seed and Orange Whirls

This recipe shows another great way of adding extra interest to **bought puff pastry** – by rolling a well-flavoured filling between the layers before baking. These are best served freshly baked.

4 tablespoons poppy seeds
finely grated zest of 1 unwaxed orange
4 tablespoons light muscovado sugar
350g bought puff pastry block
25g unsalted butter, very soft
beaten egg, to glaze
3 tablespoons orange marmalade

1. Preheat the oven to 200°C (180°C fan), 400°F, Gas 6. **Line** a baking sheet with baking paper and position the metal baking rings on the paper.

2. Combine the poppy seeds, orange zest and sugar in a small bowl, working the ingredients together with the back of a dessertspoon so they're thoroughly mixed.

3. **Roll** out the pastry on a lightly floured surface to a 35 x 20cm rectangle. Try and keep the sides of the pastry as square as you can by rolling up and down the dough, or across, rather than diagonally. Cut the rectangle in half lengthways. Dot one half with the soft butter, spreading it with a knife until fairly evenly covered. Scatter with the poppy seed mixture, spreading it as evenly as you can. Position the second pastry rectangle on top and press the rolling pin into the surface of the dough all along its length to squash the filling into the pastry. Roll the pastry, cautiously at first so the filling doesn't spill out, to a rectangle measuring 40 x 26cm. Cut lengthways into eight even-sized strips.

4. Take one strip and twist one end in one direction and the other in the opposite direction to form a loose twist. Starting at one end roll the coil up loosely on the surface until you have a round pastry shape. Drop this into one of the metal rings and repeat with the remaining strips.

5. Brush with beaten egg to **glaze** and bake for 15–20 minutes until risen and golden. While they are in the oven, make a marmalade glaze by pressing the marmalade through a small sieve into a bowl and stirring in 1 teaspoon boiling water from the kettle. Lift the rings from the pastries and brush the tops with the glaze. Serve freshly baked.

Easy does it

HANDS-ON TIME:
20 minutes

BAKING TIME:
15–20 minutes

MAKES:
8 pastries

SPECIAL EQUIPMENT:
large baking sheet, 8 × 9cm metal baking rings (or use 4 rings and bake in 2 batches)

PASTRY USED:
Bought puff, page 32

STORAGE:
Serve still warm or store for up to 1 day in an airtight container and warm through in a moderate oven for 10 minutes

Smoked Salmon, Dill and Caper Vol au Vents

Use **bought puff pastry** to practise making your own vol au vent cases. For a more ambitious version substitute your own home-made puff pastry (see page 26).

500g bought puff pastry block
1 egg yolk, to glaze

For the filling
75g good-quality mayonnaise
50g Greek yoghurt

3 tablespoons chopped dill
1 tablespoon capers, rinsed and chopped
200g smoked salmon
freshly ground black pepper
sprigs of dill, to garnish

1. Preheat the oven to 230°C (210°C fan), 450°F, Gas 8 and **line** a baking sheet with baking paper. **Roll** out the pastry on a lightly floured surface to 6mm thickness. This is very thick for puff pastry but is worth measuring accurately with a ruler. Too thin and you won't have enough cavity for filling – too thick and they'll topple over in the oven.

2. Using the large 5cm pastry cutter, stamp out 16 rounds and transfer to the baking sheet. You can re-roll the trimmings to make more, though these won't be as perfectly shaped as the first roll and will probably lose their shape during baking. **Chill** the pastries for 5 minutes in the freezer or 10 minutes in the fridge. While chilling, beat the egg yolk with 1 teaspoon water ready for glazing.

3. Press the smaller 3cm cutter into the centre of the pastries to mark out the cavity, making sure you don't cut right through. Using a paintbrush, brush the outer circle of the pastry tops with egg yolk to **glaze**. Take care not to get any egg down the cut sides or it'll bake the layers together and cause uneven rising. Bake for 12–15 minutes until risen and deep golden.

4. Leave to stand for 5 minutes then cut through the marked inner circle with the tip of a knife and ease out and discard the centres of the pastries, including some of the soft pastry dough inside. Transfer the vol au vents to a wire rack to cool.

5. While the pastries are cooling, make the filling. Put the mayonnaise, yoghurt, dill and capers in a medium bowl and mix together. Cut the smoked salmon into small dice and add to the bowl with plenty of freshly ground black pepper. Spoon into the cooled pastries with a small teaspoon, piling the filling up a little above the rims. Serve garnished with sprigs of dill.

Try Something Different

For an alternative filling, beat 1 tablespoon sun-dried tomato pesto and a good pinch of paprika into 75g mayonnaise. Add 250g smoked chicken, cut into 1cm dice, 5 tablespoons double cream and the diced flesh of 3 tomatoes. Season to taste and spoon into the cases. Serve garnished with small basil leaves.

HANDS-ON TIME:
35 minutes, plus chilling and cooling

BAKING TIME:
12–15 minutes

MAKES:
16 vol au vents

SPECIAL EQUIPMENT:
large baking sheet, 5cm and 3cm round pastry cutters, fine paintbrush

PASTRY USED:
Bought puff, page 32

STORAGE:
Keep the unfilled pastries in an airtight container for up to 3 days. Warm through in a moderate oven before filling on the day of serving

Blueberry and Lemon Financiers

A familiar sight in a French patisserie, financiers are made using an almondy batter for a moist texture that benefits from overnight chilling before baking. The batter is made with browned ·butter, which gives a slightly nuttier flavour.

100g unsalted butter, diced
100g ground almonds
2 tablespoons cornflour
125g icing sugar
finely grated zest of 1 unwaxed lemon
pinch of salt
4 medium egg whites, at room temperature

30g flaked almonds
125g blueberries

For the icing
1½ teaspoons lemon juice
50g icing sugar

Easy does it

HANDS-ON TIME:
15 minutes

BAKING TIME:
15–17 minutes

MAKES:
8 cakes

SPECIAL EQUIPMENT:
8 × 150ml individual loaf tins

STORAGE:
keep in an airtight container, in a single layer, for up to 2 days

1. Put the butter into a small pan and heat gently until the butter has melted and is beginning to foam. Continue to cook for another 2–3 minutes until the butter starts to turn golden and has a slightly nutty aroma. Remove from the heat and leave to cool completely. To speed things up, pour the butter out onto a dinner plate so it cools quickly.

2. Combine the ground almonds, cornflour, icing sugar, lemon zest and salt in a large bowl. Add the egg whites and stir the ingredients together with a wooden spoon to combine. Once the mixture is loosened, start using a whisk to beat the mixture until you have a thick paste. Pour in the cooled browned butter and stir again to make a smooth batter. Cover the bowl with clingfilm and **chill** in the fridge for at least 2 hours or overnight.

3. Preheat the oven to 200°C (180°C fan), 400°F, Gas 6. **Grease** the bases and sides of the loaf tins with butter. **Line** the bases and long sides of the tins with baking paper, and grease the paper.

4. Using a dessertspoon, spoon the batter into the tins, filling them no more than half-full. Sprinkle with the flaked almonds and then the blueberries. Bake for 15–17 minutes until the cakes have risen and feel just firm to the touch. They should be pale golden around the edges. Leave in the tins for 5 minutes then loosen the edges with a knife and transfer to a wire rack to cool.

5. Put the lemon juice in a small bowl and beat in the icing sugar until you have a smooth icing that leaves a ribbon-like trail when the spoon is lifted. Add a drop or two more water if the icing is too thick. Drizzle teaspoonfuls of the icing back and forth across the cakes.

Try Something Different

For a dairy-free alternative, make the recipe as above but use dairy-free spread in place of the butter. Ring the changes with flavour by adding the finely grated zest of 1 orange, or a few drops of rosewater or coconut extract.

Mini Pissaladières

Traditionally made using a yeasted dough, this version of a classic French pissaladière tastes just as good using a light and buttery soured cream pastry. These make an impressive starter or light snack for entertaining.

For the pastry
200g plain flour
125g chilled unsalted butter, diced
pinch of salt
5 tablespoons sowed cream

For the filling
4 tablespoons olive oil

400g red onions, thinly sliced
1 tablespoon finely chopped oregano, plus a few leaves to garnish
beaten egg, to glaze
50g pitted black olives, halved
50g anchovies in oil, drained
freshly ground black pepper

HANDS-ON TIME:
30 minutes, plus chilling and cooling

BAKING TIME:
20 minutes

MAKES:
8 pissaladières

SPECIAL EQUIPMENT:
2 baking sheets

STORAGE:
Serve freshly baked or make ahead and open freeze, layering in a freezer bag or rigid container once solid. Bake from frozen in a moderate oven for about 20 minutes.

1. To make the pastry, put the flour and butter in a large bowl with the salt. **Rub in** until you have a mix of fine and coarse crumbs. Stir in the soured cream and 2 tablespoons cold water and mix with a round-bladed knife until the mixture starts to **form** a dough. If the dough feels dry and crumbly, add a dash more water. Gather the dough together with your hands and turn it out onto the surface. Bring together into a fairly smooth dough, working the dough as little as possible to avoid toughening the pastry. **Shape** into a block, wrap in clingfilm and **chill** in the freezer for 15 minutes or the fridge for 30 minutes.

2. While the pastry is chilling, make a start on the filling. Heat the oil in a frying pan. Add the onions and fry gently, stirring frequently, for 12–15 minutes until soft and deep golden. Stir in the oregano and leave to cool.

3. Preheat the oven to 200°C (180°C fan), 400°F, Gas 6 and **line** two baking sheets with baking paper. Cut the dough into 8 even-sized pieces. Take one piece and **roll** it out on a lightly floured surface, rotating the pastry as you roll, until it is roughly round and about 14cm in diameter. Fold over the edge of the round and press firmly into the pastry base until you've made a tart case of about 10cm in diameter with a shallow rim. Repeat with the remaining pastry to make eight cases. Place on the baking sheets.

4. Brush the edges of the pastry with beaten egg to **glaze.** Stir the olives into the onion mixture and spoon into the cases, spreading it up to the rims. Cut the anchovies in half lengthways and cross two lengths over each tart. Grind over some black pepper. Bake for 20 minutes, until the pastry is puffed and golden. Serve warm or at room temperature with fresh oregano on top.

Try Something Different

If you're not fond of anchovies, stir 2 teaspoons of chopped capers or 3 sun-dried tomatoes in oil, drained and finely shredded, into the onion mixture.

Palmiers with Gingerbread Spices

Home-made **rough puff pastry**
makes light, buttery pastry, perfect
for these classic French pastry treats.
The addition of three traditional
gingerbread spices gives them an
interesting twist.

Easy does it

HANDS-ON TIME:
50 minutes, plus
chilling

BAKING TIME:
15–18 minutes

MAKES:
about 40 pastries

SPECIAL
EQUIPMENT:
2 large baking sheets

PASTRY USED:
Rough puff, page 32

STORAGE:
Keep for up to
5 days in an airtight
container

For the rough puff pastry
200g strong white bread flour
140g chilled unsalted butter, cut into
1.5cm cubes
pinch of salt
2 teaspoons lemon juice
110ml cold water

For the filling
50g caster sugar
1 teaspoon each of ground cinnamon,
ginger and allspice

To finish
50g dark chocolate, preferably a
minimum of 70 per cent cocoa solids,
melted

1. First make the rough puff pastry.
Put the flour in a bowl with the butter
and salt. Stir with a round-bladed knife
until the butter is coated in flour. Cut
through the butter several times with
the knife to break it into smaller pieces,
but still keeping it in lumps. Add the
lemon juice and cold water. Mix to
form a fairly soft but not sticky dough.
If there's dry flour in the bottom of
the bowl, stir in another 2–3 teaspoons
cold water.

2. Gather the dough together into
a ball and turn out onto a floured
surface. The dough will look very
shaggy and lumpy. **Shape** the dough
with your hands into a small, fat
rectangle ready for rolling.

3. You're going to **roll** out the dough
several times. First roll out the dough
with short, sharp movements, using a
well-floured rolling pin, until you have a
rectangle measuring about 40 x 15cm
with one short end facing you. Fold the
bottom third of the pastry up and then
the top third down over the folded

piece to make a square of three layers.
Brush off any excess lumps of flour that
have collected using a pastry brush. Press
the edges of the pastry with a rolling
pin to seal and trap in more air. Give the
square a quarter turn clockwise.
Continued

4. Press the rolling pin across the square two or three times to make indents and flatten the dough slightly. Repeat the rolling, folding and sealing of the edges as you did the first time, keeping everything well floured. Give the dough a quarter turn clockwise, then wrap in clingfilm, remembering which is the front edge. **Chill** for no longer than 15 minutes in the freezer. This will help firm up the butter before rolling again and is quicker than chilling it in the fridge. Put the timer on so you don't forget it.

5. Roll, fold and seal the dough twice more (there's no need to chill it again). The butter might start to soften and stick, in which case just liberally flour the surface and rolling pin. The dough should now be looking quite smooth.

If it's still streaky and uneven looking, give it one more roll and fold. Wrap and chill the dough for 1 hour.

6. Combine the 50g sugar with 1 teaspoon each of ground cinnamon, ginger and allspice in a small bowl. Sprinkle half onto the worktop and place the block of dough on top. Roll the dough until twice its previous size then spread the remaining sugar over the surface.

7. Continue to roll out the dough until you have a 45cm square and the dough is just 2mm thick and coated in a fine layer of spiced sugar. Try to keep the edges neat and straight as you roll by always rolling up and down, or across the dough rather than diagonally. Trim off any uneven edges with a knife.

8. Mark a line down the centre of the dough without cutting through it. Fold over one outside edge until it almost meets the central mark. Fold over the edge on the other side until it too almost meets the central mark. Fold the edges in again so you have four layers of pastry on either side of the mark. Bring the two sides together to create a flat log of eight layers of pastry. Cut in half widthways and wrap in clingfilm. Freeze for 30 minutes to firm up.

9. Preheat the oven to 190°C (170°C fan), 375°F, Gas 5 and **line** two baking sheets with baking paper. Cut the pastries across into 1cm thick slices and space at least 8cm apart on the baking sheets, cut sides face up. Bake for 15–18 minutes until crisp and pale golden. Transfer to a wire rack to cool.

10. When the pastries are completely cool, use a teaspoon to drizzle melted chocolate in zigzag lines over the top of the pastries.

Try Something Different

For a simpler variation use 450g bought puff pastry instead of the rough puff and use 2½ teaspoons ground mixed spice instead of the gingerbread spices.

Lemon Thyme Madeleines

Madeleines are a great way to practise the **whisked sponge** technique. You'll need a specialist madeleine tray to bake them in to get their classic shell shapes.

100g unsalted butter
125g golden caster sugar
3 medium eggs, at room temperature
1 tablespoon finely chopped lemon thyme

finely grated zest of 1 unwaxed lemon
125g plain flour, plus extra for dusting
pinch of salt
90g icing sugar
2½–3 teaspoons lemon juice

Easy does it

HANDS-ON TIME:
25 minutes, plus chilling

BAKING TIME:
20–25 minutes

MAKES:
24–30 madeleines

SPECIAL EQUIPMENT:
metal or silicone 12-hole madeleine tray

METHOD USED:
Whisked sponge, page 29

STORAGE:
Best served freshly baked

1. **Grease** the madeleine tray holes by brushing them with a little melted butter. Dust with flour and tip out the excess. Melt the butter gently in a small pan and leave to cool.

2. Put the sugar, eggs, lemon thyme and lemon zest in a large bowl and **whisk** using a hand-held electric whisk for 6–8 minutes until the mixture is very thick and pale. The whisk should leave a thick ribbon-like trail when lifted.

3. Sift the flour into the bowl and gently **fold** in using a large metal spoon. Drizzle the melted butter over the mixture and carefully fold in using the metal spoon until no streaks of butter remain. Be very gentle with the mixture at this stage – you don't want to lose all the air you've incorporated. The mixture can be cooked straight away but to achieve the classic 'hump' of a traditional madeleine it's best to **chill** the mixture for at least 3 hours. Alternatively you can chill the mixture in the fridge overnight before baking. Preheat the oven to 200°C (180°C fan), 400°F, Gas 6.

4. Spoon a little mixture into each of the madeleine moulds until about two-thirds full; adjust as needed as mould sizes vary. (You'll need to bake them in batches.) There's no need to spread the mixture out, it'll do this as it bakes. Bake for 7–8 minutes, or until risen and golden. The sponge should spring back when gently pressed in the middle. Stand the tray on a wire rack and leave to cool and firm up for a couple of minutes, then tip out the madeleines onto the wire rack and leave to cool. Wipe out the moulds, re-grease and flour and cook the remaining mixture in the same way.

5. While the madeleines are still warm, make the **glaze**. Put 2½ teaspoons of the lemon juice in a small bowl and beat in the icing sugar to make a thin paste. It should coat the back of the spoon – add the remaining lemon juice if it seems too thick. Arrange the madeleines, shell sides up, on the wire rack and place the rack over some baking paper to catch any drips. Use a pastry brush to brush the glaze over the shell sides and serve within 4–5 hours.

Try Something Different

Try other flavourings such as 1 teaspoon finely chopped rosemary or 2 teaspoons finely chopped lavender flowers. For a less sweet variation dust the madeleines with icing sugar instead of using the glaze.

Salted Pecan Tartlets

These delicious little treats are made using **pâte sablée**, used in pastries and delicate biscuits where a crisp snap is required. Unlike most tarts, these are not baked blind because the nutty filling holds the pastry in place without making the base soggy.

For the pâte sablée
125g unsalted butter, softened
80g golden icing sugar
1 medium egg yolk
200g plain flour
pinch of salt

For the pecan filling
125g pecan nuts
12 rounded teaspoons ready-made caramel spread
¼ teaspoon sea salt flakes

Easy does it

HANDS-ON TIME:
30 minutes, plus chilling

BAKING TIME:
22 minutes

MAKES:
12 tartlets

SPECIAL EQUIPMENT:
12-hole shallow bun tin, 7cm round, plain or fluted pastry cutter

PASTRY USED:
Pâte sablée, page 23

STORAGE:
Keep in an airtight container for up to 2 days

1. To make the pâte sablée, put the butter and sugar in a medium bowl and beat with a hand-held electric whisk for about 5 minutes until pale and creamy. Add the egg yolk and beat until combined. Add the flour and salt and mix together on a low speed until the mixture starts to clump together in large pieces. At this stage use your hands to **form** the mixture into a compact dough.

2. Turn out onto a lightly floured surface and **knead** into a smooth ball. Take care not to over-work the mixture. It just needs to be smooth and uniform. **Shape** into a block, wrap in clingfilm and **chill** in the freezer for 15 minutes or the fridge for 30 minutes.

3. Preheat the oven to 180°C (160°C fan), 350°F, Gas 4. **Roll** out the dough on a lightly floured surface to the thickness of a £1 coin (about 2–3mm). Stamp out 12 rounds using the pastry cutter and use to **line** the tin sections. Lightly prick the bases with a fork.

(Gather up the trimmings into a ball and freeze for a smaller batch of tartlets another time.) Chill the tin in the fridge for 15 minutes.

4. Halve the nuts lengthways and place in the tartlet cases. Bake for 15 minutes until the pastry is pale golden and looks cooked. Remove from the oven and spoon one rounded teaspoonful of the caramel onto the centre of each tartlet. Press the sea salt between your thumb and forefinger to crush the flakes. Sprinkle just a few little pieces over each tartlet. Return to the oven for a further 6–7 minutes until the caramel has melted and is bubbling around the edges. Leave in the tin for 10 minutes then loosen the edges with the tip of a knife and transfer to a wire rack to cool.

Portuguese Custard Tarts

These creamy, vanilla custard tarts show an unusual and effective technique for making **puff pastry** cases. Cornflour is used to thicken the custard, giving it the authentic, creamy consistency of the custard tarts sold in Portugal.

280g bought puff pastry block (or make your own, see page 26)
4 medium egg yolks
1 teaspoon vanilla extract

75g caster sugar
2 tablespoons cornflour
400ml single cream
good pinch of ground cinnamon

Easy does it

HANDS-ON TIME:
35 minutes

BAKING TIME:
about 30 minutes

MAKES:
12 tarts

SPECIAL EQUIPMENT:
12-hole deep muffin tray

PASTRY USED:
Bought puff, page 32

STORAGE:
Keep in an airtight container in a cool place for up to 2 days

1. Preheat the oven to 200°C (180°C fan), 400°F, Gas 6. Generously **grease** the holes of the muffin tray and chill in the fridge.

2. **Roll** out the pastry on a lightly floured surface to about 30 x 20cm (there's no need to be too accurate as the pastry will be further rolled and shaped). Roll up the pastry tightly, starting from a short side until you have a narrow log shape. Cut the log across into 12 even-sized pieces; cut in half first, then into quarters and then each quarter into three.

3. Take one piece and roll it on a lightly floured surface, cut side face down, to a circle about 10cm in diameter. Fit into one tin hole, pressing it up the sides until it sits level with the top of the hole. Use your fingers to mould the pastry, pressing it around the sides of the mould, making sure there are no cracks. Repeat with the remaining holes. Prick the bases lightly with a fork.

4. Cut twelve 14cm squares of foil and use to **line** the pastry cases. The easiest way to do this is to crease the foil square around a small fruit such as a lemon and push into one of the

pastry cases. Remove the lemon and push the sides of the foil out so it fits the pastry case snugly with no gaps. Repeat with the rest. Fill with baking beans or uncooked rice and **blind bake** for 12 minutes until the pastry is cooked enough to hold its shape. Remove from the oven and lift out the foil and beans.

5. Put the egg yolks, vanilla extract, caster sugar and cornflour in a large, wide jug. Beat with a wooden spoon until smooth.

6. Pour the single cream into a pan and add a good pinch of cinnamon. Place over a medium heat until just before it starts to boil. Pour into the egg yolk mixture, stirring until smooth. Pour the custard into the pastry cases, leaving a pastry rim of about 5mm. Sprinkle with a pinch more cinnamon.

7. Bake for 18–20 minutes until the pastry is pale golden and the custard still has a slight wobble in the centre. Leave in the tray for 10 minutes then transfer to a wire rack. Serve warm or at room temperature.

Mini Victoria Sandwich Cakes with Tropical Fruits

These individual sandwich cakes are made using the creamed cake method. A fruity filling of mango and passion fruit gives them a vibrant, tropical twist.

HANDS-ON TIME:
35 minutes, plus cooling

BAKING TIME:
17–20 minutes

MAKES:
12 cakes

SPECIAL EQUIPMENT:
12-hole deep muffin tray

STORAGE:
Best eaten on the day of making, or make the sponge a day in advance and keep in an airtight container before filling and serving

For the sponge

3 medium eggs, at room temperature
about 175g unsalted butter, softened
about 175g golden caster sugar
1 teaspoon vanilla extract
about 175g self-raising flour
1 tablespoon lukewarm tap water

For the filling

2 passion fruit
1 large mango, peeled and cut into small dice
1 teaspoon lime juice
150ml double cream, well chilled
2 tablespoons icing sugar, plus extra for dusting

1. Preheat the oven to 180°C (160°C fan), 350°F, Gas 4. **Grease** the holes of the muffin tray with butter and **line** the bases with baking paper. Weigh the eggs – they should weigh about 175g in their shells – then use the same weight for the butter, sugar and flour.

2. Put the butter in a large bowl or the bowl of a free-standing mixer and beat with the whisk attachment or hand-held electric whisk until soft and creamy. Scrape down the sides of the bowl with a plastic spatula, then gradually beat in the sugar, a couple of tablespoons at a time. Scrape the mixture from the sides again and beat well for 1 minute or until the mixture looks very light and fluffy.

3. Lightly beat the eggs in a jug with the vanilla extract. Add to the butter mixture a tablespoon at a time, beating well after each addition and scraping down the sides of the bowl. If the mixture looks like it might be 'splitting', stir in a tablespoon of the flour.

4. Sift the remainder of the flour into the bowl. Start to gently **fold** in the flour with a large metal spoon. After two or three movements add the warm water.

Keep folding in until the flour is well mixed in and there are no streaks.

5. Spoon the mixture into the holes of the muffin tray, no more than two-thirds full. Bake for 17–20 minutes until light golden brown and just beginning to shrink away from the sides of the tin. Remove from the oven and gently run a knife around the outside of each cake to loosen. Rest a cooling rack over the tin and invert the cakes onto the rack. Lift away the tin, peel away the paper and turn the cakes the right way up. Leave to cool completely.

6. Halve the passion fruit and scoop the pulp into a small bowl. Put the diced mango in another small bowl with the lime juice and 2 teaspoons of the passion fruit pulp.

7. Put the cream, icing sugar and the rest of the passion fruit pulp in a bowl. **Whip** with a hand-held electric whisk to **soft peaks**. Cut each cake horizontally in half with a small serrated knife. Spoon the cream onto the bases, spreading to the edges. Pile the mango mixture over the cream. Finish with the sponge tops and dust with icing sugar.

Frangipane Barquettes

Barquettes are small boat-shaped tartlets – 'barque' is the French word for boat. This recipe is a good introduction to making, rolling and shaping **pâte sucrée**, a delicious dessert pastry, used extensively in patisserie recipes.

For the pâte sucrée

60g unsalted butter, at room temperature
25g golden caster sugar
1 medium egg yolk
100g plain flour

For the filling

50g unsalted butter, softened

50g golden caster sugar
1 medium egg
½ teaspoon almond extract
50g ground almonds
1 tablespoon plain flour
2 small fresh figs, each cut into 6 wedges
3 tablespoons apricot jam

HANDS-ON TIME:
40 minutes, plus chilling and cooling

BAKING TIME:
16–18 minutes

MAKES:
12 barquettes

SPECIAL EQUIPMENT:
12 barquette tins, each 9.5–10cm in length, baking sheet

PASTRY USED:
Pâte sucrée, page 22

STORAGE:
Keep in an airtight container in a cool place for up to 2 days before glazing the figs

1. First make the pastry. Cream the butter and sugar in a bowl with a wooden spoon. Beat in the egg yolk. Stir in the flour, a third at a time, then work the mixture together with your fingertips, along with 1 teaspoon of cold water (add a drop more if needed), until it starts to clump together and **form** a dough. Tip the dough onto the work surface and **knead** very briefly until smooth. Wrap in clingfilm and **chill** for 15 minutes in the freezer or 30 minutes in the fridge.

2. **Roll** out the pastry on a lightly floured surface to a thickness of 2mm. Using a barquette tin as a guide, **cut out** the pastry at least 2cm larger than the size of the tin. **Line** the tin, pressing the pastry gently up the sides. Trim off the excess with a sharp knife. Line the remaining tins in the same way (re-roll the trimmings). Prick the bases with a fork and chill while you make the filling.

3. Put the butter and sugar in a small bowl and beat with a wooden spoon to make a smooth paste. Beat in the egg, almond extract, ground almonds and flour until evenly combined.

4. Preheat the oven to 200°C (180°C fan), 400°F, Gas 6 and put a baking sheet in the oven to heat up. Place ¼ teaspoon apricot jam in each pastry case and spread over the base. Spoon the almond mixture on top, spreading it to the edges, to cover the jam. The filling shouldn't come above the pastry rim or it might spill over during baking.

5. Bake the pastries for 10 minutes until the filling is just about set but not golden. Arrange a fig wedge on top of each pastry and return to the oven for a further 6–8 minutes until the tarts are golden. Leave in the tins for 5 minutes before loosening the edges with the tip of a sharp knife and transferring to a wire rack to cool.

6. Press the remaining jam through a sieve into a small pan. Add 2 teaspoons water and heat gently until the jam has softened. Brush over the figs.

Black Forest Meringues

These craggy, freeform meringues are rippled with cherry conserve and sandwiched in pairs with home-made chocolate ganache, a widely used filling and topping in so many baking recipes.

HANDS-ON TIME:
35 minutes, plus cooling

BAKING TIME:
1¼ hours

MAKES:
about 10 meringues

SPECIAL EQUIPMENT:
2 baking sheets

TECHNIQUE USED:
French meringue, page 31

STORAGE:
Best served freshly baked

65g black cherry conserve
3 medium egg whites, at room temperature
pinch of salt
¼ teaspoon cream of tartar
175g caster sugar

75g good-quality dark chocolate, preferably a minimum of 70 per cent cocoa solids, broken into pieces
75ml double cream
1 tablespoon light muscovado sugar

1. Preheat the oven to 120°C (100°C fan), 250°F, Gas ½ and line two baking sheets with baking paper. Put the cherry conserve in a small bowl and mix well to soften.

2. To make the meringue, put the egg whites, salt and cream of tartar in a large, spotlessly clean bowl. Gently whisk using a hand-held electric whisk to break up the egg whites. Increase the speed and whisk until the mixture stands in soft peaks when the whisk is lifted from the bowl. Add a rounded tablespoon of the sugar and whisk for a further 15 seconds. Add another spoonful of the sugar and whisk again. Continue to whisk in the sugar, a tablespoon at a time, until the meringue is thick and glossy. It's really important not to add the sugar too quickly as the egg whites won't be able to hold it and the sugar syrup will seep out during baking.

3. Using a teaspoon, drizzle half the cherry conserve over the meringue. Turn a large metal spoon through the conserve two or three times as though folding in. This is just to ripple the conserve into the meringue but not to completely combine it. Dot the remaining conserve over the meringue and cut through again. Take heaped dessertspoonfuls of the meringue and place on the baking sheets spacing them slightly apart. There should be 20.

4. Bake for about 1¼ hours, or until the meringues are crisp and dry and can be lifted easily from the paper. Leave to cool on the paper.

5. To make the ganache, put the chocolate in a heatproof bowl. Heat the cream and sugar gently in a small pan until the sugar has dissolved and the cream is almost coming to the boil. Immediately remove from the heat and pour the hot cream over the chocolate. Leave to stand for a few minutes until the chocolate has melted, stirring occasionally. Leave to cool for about 1 hour until the mixture is thick enough to hold its shape.

6. Place a little of the ganache onto the flat base of a meringue and spread it almost to the edges with a palette knife. Position another meringue on top, pressing down very gently. Repeat with the remainder and leave in a cool place for about an hour to let the ganache firm up before serving.

Cranberry and Almond Eccles Cakes

Here, home-made **rough puff pastry** is flavoured with ginger and cinnamon for a really spicy twist. The lattice design is incredibly effective and requires no special equipment.

HANDS-ON TIME:
50 minutes, plus chilling

BAKING TIME:
20–25 minutes

MAKES:
16 Eccles cakes

SPECIAL EQUIPMENT:
large baking sheet

PASTRY USED:
Rough puff pastry, see page 24

STORAGE:
Keep in an airtight container for up to 3 days. Can be warmed through to serve

For the rough puff pastry
225g strong white bread flour
1 teaspoon ground ginger
1 teaspoon ground cinnamon
160g chilled unsalted butter, cut into 1.5cm cubes
pinch of salt
2 teaspoons lemon juice

For the filling
100g dried cranberries
50g flaked almonds
65g light muscovado sugar
75g sultanas
finely grated zest of 1 unwaxed orange
beaten egg, to glaze
caster sugar, to sprinkle

1. First make the rough puff pastry. Put the flour and spices in a bowl with the butter and salt. Stir with a round-bladed knife until the butter is coated in flour. Cut through the butter several times with the knife to break it into smaller pieces, but still keeping it in lumps. Pour in the lemon juice and 110ml cold water. Mix to **form** a fairly soft but not sticky dough. If there's dry flour in the bottom of the bowl, stir in another 2–3 teaspoons cold water.

2. Gather the dough together into a ball and turn out onto a floured surface. The dough will look very shaggy and lumpy until it's rolled several times. **Shape** the dough with your hands into a small, fat rectangle ready for rolling.

3. You're going to **roll** out the dough several times. First roll out the dough with short, sharp movements, using a well-floured rolling pin, until you have a rectangle measuring about 40 × 15cm with one short end facing you. Fold the bottom third of the pastry up and then the top third down over the folded piece to make a square of three layers.

Brush off any excess lumps of flour that have collected using a pastry brush. Press the edges of the pastry with a rolling pin to seal and trap in more air. Give the square a quarter turn clockwise.

4. Press the rolling pin across the square two or three times to make indents and flatten the dough slightly. Repeat the rolling, folding and sealing of the edges as you did the first time, keeping everything well floured. Give the dough a quarter turn clockwise, then wrap in clingfilm, remembering which is the front edge. **Chill** for no longer than 15 minutes in the freezer. This will help firm up the butter before rolling again and is quicker than chilling it in the fridge. Put the timer on so you don't forget it.
Continued

5. Roll, fold and seal the dough twice more (there's no need to chill it again). The butter might start to soften and stick, in which case just liberally flour the surface and rolling pin. The dough should now be looking quite smooth. If it's still streaky and uneven looking, give it one more roll and fold. Wrap and chill the dough for 1 hour.

6. While chilling, combine the filling ingredients so they're ready and waiting. Put the 100g cranberries, 50g flaked almonds, 65g light muscovado sugar, 75g sultanas and zest of 1 orange in a bowl and mix well.

7. Preheat the oven to 200°C (180°C fan), 400°F, Gas 6 and **line** a baking sheet with baking paper. Roll out the pastry on a lightly floured surface to a 40cm square. Cut into four 10cm strips, then cut across all the strips to create sixteen 10cm squares.

8. Make three 2cm cuts down the centre of one square, leaving a 5mm gap between the cuts. Make three more rows of cuts, either side of the first so you end up with a staggered arrangement of cuts. Repeat with the remaining squares.

9. Brush the edges of the squares with beaten egg and spoon the filling into the centres. Bring the edges of one pastry square up over the filling, pinching them firmly together to seal.

10. Turn over onto one baking sheet and flatten with the palm of your hand so the lattice decoration shows. Repeat with the remainder.

11. Brush the pastry with more beaten egg to **glaze** and sprinkle lightly with caster sugar. Bake for 20–25 minutes until slightly risen and golden. Serve warm or cold.

Try Something Different

For more traditional Eccles cakes replace the cranberries with currants and the flaked almonds with chopped mixed peel. You could also mix a little grated unwaxed orange zest with the caster sugar before sprinkling over the pastries before baking.

English Maids
of Honour Tart

The 'grated butter' pastry technique used here gives a fabulously flaky, light crust. This prettily decorated tart makes an innovative twist on the traditional Maids of Honour recipe.

Easy does it

HANDS-ON TIME:
30 minutes, plus
chilling and cooling

BAKING TIME:
45 minutes

SERVES:
6

SPECIAL
EQUIPMENT:
baking sheet,
20cm round loose-
bottomed tart tin,
3cm deep

STORAGE:
Keep in an airtight
container in a cool
place and use within
2 days

For the pastry
175g plain flour
pinch of salt
115g chilled unsalted butter
1 egg yolk, to glaze

For the filling
2 medium eggs, at room temperature
250g curd cheese
100g caster sugar
100g ground almonds
1 teaspoon rosewater
50g raisins

1. For the pastry, put the flour and salt in a large bowl. Add the butter to the bowl in one block and coat in the flour. Lift up the block and grate a little into the bowl. Dip the block back into the flour again to coat. Continue to grate the butter into the bowl, frequently coating the whole piece in the flour and turning the grated butter into the flour to coat. This will stop the butter caking together.

2. Drizzle 5 tablespoons cold water into the bowl and stir with a round-bladed knife until the dough clumps together. Continue to bring the ingredients together to **form** a soft ball of dough using your hands. Avoid over-working the dough or it'll lose its flakiness. Turn out onto the surface, **shape** into a neat block and wrap in clingfilm. **Chill** in the freezer for 15 minutes, or the fridge for 30 minutes to firm up.

3. Preheat the oven to 200°C (180°C fan), 350°F, Gas 6 and put a baking sheet in the oven to heat up. Reserve a quarter of the pastry and **roll** out the remainder on a lightly floured surface to 3mm thickness.

Continued

4. Use to **line** the tart tin, pressing the pastry into the corners and up the sides. Trim off the excess pastry around the top and add the trimmings to the reserved dough. Prick the base lightly with a fork and chill for 15 minutes.

5. Line the pastry case with baking paper then fill with baking beans or uncooked rice. Place on the hot baking sheet and **blind bake** for 15 minutes. Remove the paper and beans and bake for a further 5 minutes. Remove and lower the oven temperature to 180°C (160°C fan), 350°F, Gas 4.

6. For the filling, beat the 2 eggs in a medium bowl to break up. Add the 250g curd cheese, 100g caster sugar, 100g ground almonds, 1 teaspoon rosewater and 50g raisins and beat with a whisk until evenly combined and lump-free. Pour the filling into the pastry case and bake for 10 minutes. Beat the 1 egg yolk in a small bowl with 1 teaspoon cold water.

7. While the tart is in the oven, roll out the reserved pastry on a lightly floured surface to 5mm thickness. **Cut out** three thin strips and two or three thicker strips, 1.5cm wide. Make diagonal cuts across these thicker strips to create simple leaf shapes. Make leaf vein marks on each with the back of a knife.

8. Remove the tart from the oven and brush the edges with the egg yolk. Take one of the long strips of pastry and rest it in a curvy line over the filling. Arrange the two other strips elsewhere on the filling. Brush with egg yolk. Arrange the leaf shapes against the curved strips and brush these with more egg yolk. Return to the oven for a further 25 minutes or until the pastry is deep golden and the filling is just firm. Serve warm or cold.

Dairy-free Butternut Squash Jalousie

A jalousie is designed to show glimpses of the appetising filling beneath the pastry. In this recipe a spicy filling is encased in a dairy-free pastry crust.

HANDS-ON TIME:
40 minutes, plus
chilling and cooling

BAKING TIME:
30 minutes

SERVES:
4

SPECIAL
EQUIPMENT:
large baking sheet

STORAGE:
Serve freshly
baked or at room
temperature, or
re-heat through in a
moderate oven for
15 minutes

For the filling
350g butternut squash, peeled and de-seeded (peeled weight), cut into dice
1 pointed red pepper, de-seeded and cut into dice
1 red onion, chopped
2 tablespoons olive oil
¼ teaspoon dried chilli flakes
2 garlic cloves, finely chopped

½ teaspoon ground cumin
4 tablespoons chopped fresh coriander
salt and freshly ground black pepper

For the pastry
250g self-raising flour
150g dairy-free spread, chilled
beaten egg, to glaze
½ teaspoon sea salt

1. Preheat the oven to 200°C (180°C fan), 400°F, Gas 6. Toss the vegetables in the oil in a roasting tin. Season with salt and pepper and roast for 50–60 minutes until soft and lightly browned. Turn once or twice during cooking so they roast evenly. Stir in the chilli flakes, garlic, cumin and coriander and roast for a further 5 minutes. Leave to cool.

2. For the pastry, put the flour in a large bowl. Add the dairy-free spread in one lump and coat in the flour. Lift out of the bowl and grate a little back into the bowl. Dip the block of spread into the bowl again to coat the grated side in flour. Continue to grate the spread into the bowl, frequently coating the whole piece in the flour. This will stop it caking together.

3. Drizzle 4 tablespoons cold water into the bowl and stir with a round-bladed knife until the dough clumps together. Bring together to **form** a soft ball of dough using your hands.

4. Turn out onto the work surface and **knead** gently into a smooth ball. Avoid over-working the dough or it'll lose its flakiness. **Shape** into a neat block and wrap in clingfilm. **Chill** in the freezer for 15 minutes, or the fridge for 30 minutes.

5. **Line** a baking sheet with baking paper. Cut the pastry in half. **Roll** out one half on a lightly floured surface and **cut out** a 28 × 16cm rectangle. Transfer to the lined baking sheet. Brush the edges with beaten egg and pile the cooled filling in the centre, leaving a 2cm border. Roll out the second half, and cut out a 30 × 16cm rectangle. Using the tip of a sharp knife, make widthways cuts through the pastry, 1cm apart and leaving a 2cm rim around the edges. Lift the pastry over the filling, using a fish slice to support one end. Seal the pastry layers firmly around the edges. Evenly space the gaps in the lid.

6. Flute the edges of the pastry by pushing the finger of one hand against the pastry and squeezing the pastry around it with the thumb and forefinger of your other hand. Brush with beaten egg to **glaze** and sprinkle with sea salt. Bake for 30 minutes until deep golden.

Vanilla Chouquettes

This recipe is good practice for more complex **choux pastry** creations. Spoonfuls of the pastry are simply spooned onto the baking sheet and sprinkled with crushed loaf sugar for flavour and texture contrast.

Easy does it

HANDS-ON TIME:
25 minutes

BAKING TIME:
30 minutes

MAKES:
22–24 chouquettes

SPECIAL EQUIPMENT:
large baking sheet

PASTRY USED:
Choux pastry,
page 28

STORAGE:
Best eaten freshly
baked

50g rough-cut sugar cubes
3 medium eggs, beaten
65g plain flour
50g unsalted butter

1 teaspoon caster sugar
pinch of salt
½ teaspoon vanilla bean paste
150ml cold water

1. Preheat the oven to 180°C (160°C fan), 350°F, Gas 4 and **line** a baking sheet with baking paper.

2. Put the sugar cubes in a polythene food bag and tap with a rolling pin until the sugar is broken into pieces, each a scant 5mm in diameter (much of the sugar will have become granulated – you'll only need the chunkier pieces) and put to one side. Beat the eggs in a bowl to break them up. Transfer 1½ tablespoons of beaten egg to a small bowl and reserve for glazing. The rest will be used in the pastry.

3. Sift the flour onto a square of baking paper. This makes it easier to tip the flour quickly into the pan in one go. Cut the butter into pieces and put in a medium pan with the caster sugar, salt, vanilla bean paste and cold water. Heat gently until the butter has melted, then increase the heat until the liquid is at a rolling boil. Immediately tip in the flour and beat with a wooden spoon to make a thick paste.

4. With the pan still on the heat, beat the paste for 1–2 minutes until it is smooth and forms a ball that leaves the sides of the pan clean. Turn into a bowl and leave until the paste stops steaming, beating frequently with a wooden spoon.

5. Add a tablespoon of the beaten egg to the bowl and beat until absorbed before adding another. Continue beating in the egg, a tablespoon at a time, until the dough is glossy and has a soft dropping consistency. You might not need all the egg.

6. Take a heaped teaspoonful of the mixture and slide it off onto one baking sheet with a second teaspoon. Repeat with the remaining dough, leaving a 3cm gap between each one.

7. Gently dab the tops of the pastry with the reserved egg to **glaze** and scatter with the sugar pieces. Bake for 30 minutes until puffed and golden. Turn off the oven and leave in the switched-off oven with the door closed for 30 minutes before transferring to a wire rack to cool.

Try Something Different

Try using 'pearl sugar' which is ready-made extra large sugar crystals available from specialist suppliers. You'll need 25g for this recipe. They're also delicious scattered with finely chopped chocolate instead of the sugar.

Passion Fruit Éclairs

This recipe takes **choux pastry** one step further by piping it, filling with a flavoured cream and spooning over a sweet but tangy fruit glaze. The result is an elegant treat for afternoon tea.

For the choux pastry
65g plain flour
50g unsalted butter
1 teaspoon caster sugar
good pinch of salt
150ml water
2 medium eggs, beaten

To finish
250ml whipping cream, well chilled
1 teaspoon vanilla extract
100g icing sugar, plus 1 teaspoon
1 large passion fruit

HANDS-ON TIME:
35 minutes, plus
cooling

BAKING TIME:
30 minutes

MAKES:
14 éclairs

SPECIAL
EQUIPMENT:
large baking sheet,
large piping bag,
1.5cm plain piping
nozzle

PASTRY USED:
Choux pastry,
page 28

STORAGE:
Serve on the day of
baking, or keep the
unfilled éclairs in an
airtight container for
up to 2 days before
filling and serving.
If softened during
storage, re-crisp in
a moderate oven for
5–10 minutes, then
cool and fill

1. Preheat the oven to 180°C (160°C fan), 350°F, Gas 4 and **line** a baking sheet with baking paper.

2. Sift the flour onto a square of baking paper. This makes it easier to tip the flour quickly into the pan in one go. Cut the butter into pieces and put in a medium pan with the sugar, salt and water. Heat gently until the butter has melted. Increase the heat until the liquid is at a rolling boil. Immediately tip in the flour and beat with a wooden spoon to make a thick paste.

3. With the pan still on the heat, beat the paste for 1–2 minutes until it is smooth and forms a ball that leaves the sides of the pan clean. Turn into a bowl and leave until the paste stops steaming, beating frequently.

4. Add a tablespoon of the beaten egg to the bowl and beat until absorbed before adding another spoonful. Continue beating in the egg until the dough is glossy and has a soft dropping consistency.
Continued

5. Put the paste in the piping bag fitted with the piping nozzle. **Pipe** 8–9cm lengths of the paste onto the baking paper. Release the pressure from the bag once you've piped the right length. You might find it easier to cut through the paste with the tip of a sharp knife so you can lift the bag away cleanly. Pipe the remainder in the same way.

6. Bake for about 30 minutes until puffed and golden. Turn off the oven and leave the pastries in the switched-off oven with the door closed for 30 minutes before transferring to a wire rack to cool completely.

7. Put the 250ml whipping cream, I teaspoon vanilla extract and I teaspoon icing sugar in a medium bowl. **Whip** with a hand-held electric whisk until the mixture forms **soft peaks** when the whisk is lifted from the bowl.

8. Using a small sharp knife (a serrated one is easiest), cut a horizontal slice through each pastry, leaving a little of it still intact. Ease open one pastry and spread a dessertspoonful of the cream along the base. Push the top down gently so the cream shows around the sides. Repeat with the remainder.

9. For the icing, rest a small sieve or tea strainer over a small bowl. Halve the passion fruit and scoop the pulp into the sieve. Press the juice through the sieve using the back of a dessertspoon. Measure 2 teaspoons of the juice into a separate bowl and add the 100g icing sugar and all the passion fruit seeds. Beat with a wooden spoon to make a smooth icing that thickly coats the back of the spoon. If the icing is too thick add more passion fruit juice or water, a drop at a time. Spoon a little icing onto each éclair and spread with the back of the spoon. Leave in a cool place until ready to serve.

Try Something Different

For chocolate éclairs, melt 100g dark chocolate in a heatproof bowl set over a pan of gently simmering water. Dice 25g unsalted butter into the chocolate and add 1 tablespoon golden syrup. Stir until smooth and spread over the filled éclairs.

Apple and Lemon Treacle Tart

Soured cream gives a simple rubbed-in pastry a crisp, flaky texture. This is a lighter version of a classic treacle tart.

For the pastry
200g plain flour
125g chilled unsalted butter, diced
pinch of salt
5 tablespoons soured cream

For the filling
finely grated zest and juice of
2 unwaxed lemons
650g Bramley apples
1 tablespoon cornflour
3 medium eggs, beaten
250g golden syrup

HANDS-ON TIME:
40 minutes, plus
chilling and cooling

BAKING TIME:
about 1 hour
10 minutes

MAKES:
8–10 slices

SPECIAL
EQUIPMENT:
baking sheet, 24cm
round loose-
bottomed tart tin,
3.5cm deep

STORAGE:
Keep for up to
2 days in an airtight
container. Serve cold
or warm through in a
moderate oven for
10 minutes

1. First make the pastry. Put the flour and butter in a large bowl with the salt. **Rub in** until you have a mix of fine and coarse crumbs. Stir in the soured cream and 1 tablespoon cold water and mix with a round-bladed knife until it starts to **form** a dough. If it feels dry and crumbly, add a dash more water. Gather it together on the work surface with your hands then bring together into a fairly smooth dough, working the dough as little as possible to avoid toughening the pastry. **Shape** into a block, wrap in clingfilm and **chill** in the freezer for 15 minutes or the fridge for 30 minutes.

2. Preheat the oven to 200°C (180°C fan), 400°F, Gas 6 and put a baking sheet in the oven to heat up. Reserve a quarter of the pastry and **roll** out the rest on a lightly floured surface to a thickness of 3mm. Use it to **line** the tart tin, pressing the pastry into the corners and up the sides. Trim off the excess pastry and add the trimmings to the reserved dough. Prick the base lightly with a fork and chill for 15 minutes.

3. Line the pastry case with baking paper then fill with baking beans or uncooked rice. Place on the hot baking sheet and **blind bake** for 15 minutes. Remove the paper and beans and bake

for a further 5 minutes. Remove from the oven and lower the temperature to 180°C (160°C fan), 350°F, Gas 4.

4. For the filling, put the lemon juice and zest in a large bowl. Peel, core and grate the apples into the bowl. Toss to coat in the lemon juice to stop them browning. Sprinkle with the cornflour and mix well. Add the eggs and golden syrup. Mix together thoroughly with a wooden spoon. Scrape the filling into the pastry case. It should come to about 5mm below the top of the pastry case.

5. Roll out the reserved pastry on a lightly floured surface to a thickness of 3mm. Cut into 1cm wide strips. Brush the edges of the pastry case and all over the rolled pastry with beaten egg to **glaze**. Lay one strip of pastry over the centre of the tart and further strips on either side. Let the ends overhang the edges and leave a 2cm gap between each one. Lay the remaining strips diagonally on top.

6. Bake for 10 minutes then cut off the overhanging pastry. Cook for a further 40 minutes until the pastry is crisp and golden and the filling just firm. Leave for 10 minutes, or serve at room temperature.

Cream Horns with Banana and Lime Chantilly

Home-made cream horns taste so much better than bought, even when using **bought puff pastry**. The technique of wrapping the moulds neatly and evenly in pastry is key to creating the perfect horn shape, but will become so much easier once you've practised a couple.

500g bought puff pastry block
beaten egg, to glaze
75g white chocolate, chopped

For the filling
3 small ripe bananas, skinned weight about 200g in total
finely grated zest of 2 limes, plus 5 teaspoons juice
225ml double cream, well chilled
3 tablespoons icing sugar, plus extra for dusting

Easy does it

HANDS-ON TIME:
45 minutes, plus cooling

BAKING TIME:
15–20 minutes

MAKES:
10 cream horns

SPECIAL EQUIPMENT:
large baking sheet, 10 metal cream horn moulds, large piping bag, large star piping nozzle

PASTRY USED:
Bought puff, page 32

STORAGE:
Keep unfilled cream horns in an airtight container for up to 24 hours. Serve on day of filling.

1. Preheat the oven to 220°C (200°C fan), 425°F, Gas 7 and **line** a baking sheet with baking paper. Generously **grease** the outsides of the cream horn moulds with very soft butter.

2. **Roll** out the pastry on a lightly floured surface to a 52 x 30cm rectangle. Try and keep the sides of the pastry as square as you can by rolling up and down the dough or across, rather than diagonally. Trim off the edges with a knife to neaten.

3. Cut the pastry lengthways into 2.5cm-wide strips, each 50cm long, so you end up with 10 strips altogether. Rest the tip of a cream horn mould over one end of a pastry strip. Pinch to secure the end of the strip around the mould and gradually roll the pastry around the mould, making sure there's a generous and even overlap of pastry as you go. Press the end of the strip down gently to seal and place on the baking sheet with the pastry end underneath. Repeat with the remaining strips.

Continued

4. Brush the pastry with beaten egg to **glaze** and bake for 15–20 minutes, or until deep golden. Remove from the oven and increase the temperature to 240°C (220°fan), 475°F, Gas 9. Leave the pastries to stand for 2 minutes then gently twist them out of the moulds, leaving the pastries on the baking sheet. Dust the pastries generously with icing sugar using a small sieve or tea strainer. Return to the oven for a further 3–5 minutes until they're partially caramelised (the pastries look particularly appetising when there are still bands of uncaramelised icing sugar on them). Transfer to a wire rack and leave to cool.

5. Heat a 5cm depth of water in a small pan until bubbling. Reduce the heat to its lowest setting. Put the 75g white chocolate in a heatproof bowl set over the pan of gently simmering water, making sure the bottom of the bowl doesn't touch the water. Once the chocolate starts to melt, turn off the heat and leave until completely melted, stirring occasionally with a teaspoon. Lift the bowl away from the pan. Use a pastry brush to brush the inside of each cream horn lightly with the melted chocolate and then leave to set while you make the filling. The chocolate will stop the pastry turning soggy as well as adding flavour. You can prepare the horns to this stage a day ahead.

6. For the filling, roughly slice the 3 bananas into a bowl, add the 5 teaspoons lime juice and mash with a fork until smooth. Press the banana purée through a coarse sieve into a bowl – don't forget to scrape off all the puree from the underside of the sieve. Add the 225ml cream and 3 tablespoons icing sugar and **whip** with a hand-held electric whisk until **soft peaks** form when you lift out the whisk.

7. Put the mixture in the piping bag fitted with the piping nozzle. **Pipe** the cream into the pastries, making sure that you pipe right into the tip of the horn so that there is filling in every bite. Finish with a small swirl of the filling at the open ends. Serve sprinkled with lime zest.

French Apple Tart

No collection of patisserie recipes would be complete without this French classic. Keep the **pâte sucrée** crisp and brittle and the filling fresh and tangy and your apple tart will compete with the best.

For the pâte sucrée
100g unsalted butter, at room temperature
40g golden caster sugar
2 medium egg yolks
175g plain flour

For the filling
800g cooking apple
4 teaspoons lemon juice
65g caster sugar, plus 1 tablespoon
good pinch of ground cloves
25g unsalted butter
2 eating apples

To glaze
4 tablespoons apricot jam

HANDS-ON TIME:
1 hour, plus chilling and cooling

BAKING TIME:
45 minutes

SERVES:
8

SPECIAL EQUIPMENT:
baking sheet,
35 × 12cm rectangular fluted loose-bottomed tart tin, 2.5cm deep

METHOD USED:
Pâte sucrée, page 22

STORAGE:
Wrap loosely in foil before glazing and keep in a cool place for up to 24 hours. Glaze before serving

1. First make the pâte sucrée. Put the butter and sugar in a bowl and cream together by beating with a wooden spoon until light and creamy. Beat in the egg yolks and then stir in the flour, about a third at a time, then work the mixture together with your fingertips, along with 1½ teaspoons of cold water (add a drop more if needed to bring the dough together), until it starts to clump together in big lumps and **form** a dough. Tip the dough onto the work surface and **knead** very briefly until smooth. Wrap in clingfilm and **chill** for 15 minutes in the freezer or 30 minutes in the fridge.

2. **Roll** out the pastry on a lightly floured surface to a long rectangular shape the thickness of a £1 coin (about 3mm). To make sure it's large enough to **line** the tin, hover the tin on top: there should be an excess of about 4cm all round for lining the sides and trimming. Lift the pastry into the tin, easing the pastry into the corners and flutes up the sides of the tin. Don't worry if the pastry cracks, you can press it back into shape with your fingers. Trim off the excess pastry around the rim. Prick the pastry base lightly with a fork and chill for 10 minutes. Preheat the oven to 200°C (180°C fan), 400°F, Gas 6 and put a baking sheet in the oven to heat up.
Continued

3. Line the pastry case with baking paper then fill with baking beans or uncooked rice. Place on the hot baking sheet and **blind bake** for 15 minutes. Remove the paper and beans and bake for a further 5 minutes until the base looks dry. Leave to cool while you prepare the filling.

4. Peel, core and thinly slice the 800g cooking apples into a pan. Stir in 2 teaspoons of the lemon juice, 65g caster sugar and a good pinch of ground cloves and cover with a lid. Cook very gently for 15 minutes, frequently stirring the apples with a wooden spoon so they soften evenly. The purée should become completely smooth. Beat in the 25g butter and leave to cool.

5. To prepare the apple slices for the topping, half-fill a bowl with water and add the remaining 2 teaspoons lemon juice. Quarter, core and thinly slice the 2 eating apples into the water.

6. Once the apple purée has cooled, turn it into the pastry case and spread in an even layer. Drain the apple slices and pat dry between layers of kitchen paper. Use to decorate the top of the tart by arranging the slices in two overlapping lines right down the length of the tart. Sprinkle with the 1 tablespoon sugar and bake in the oven for about 25 minutes, or until the apple slices are soft and just beginning to caramelise at the edges.

7. To **glaze** the tart, press the 4 tablespoons apricot jam through a small sieve into a bowl and stir in 1 teaspoon boiling water. Use a pastry brush to brush the glaze all over the apple slices and the top edges of the pastry case. Serve at room temperature with crème fraîche or lightly whipped cream.

Try Something Different

- If you don't have the rectangular tin, change the shape by baking the tart in a 23cm round plain or fluted loose-bottomed tart tin, 2.5cm deep.
- For a dairy-free version omit the butter from the apple purée and use a sweetened dairy-free pastry instead of the pâte sucrée.

French Macarons with Raspberries

Classic French macarons, crisp on the outside and soft and airy in the centre, are hugely popular at the moment. The perfectly shaped discs are achieved by using a template of circles drawn on the underside of the baking paper before piping.

Needs a little skill

HANDS-ON TIME:
45 minutes, plus standing and cooling

BAKING TIME:
10–12 minutes

MAKES:
14–16 macarons

SPECIAL EQUIPMENT:
5.5cm round pastry cutter, 2 baking sheets, large piping bag, 1cm plain nozzle, 1cm star nozzle

STORAGE:
Keep for up to 4 days in an airtight container before filling

For the macarons
90g ground almonds
90g icing sugar
100g egg white (from about 3 medium eggs), at room temperature
100g caster sugar
a little pink gel or paste food colouring

To finish
200ml whipping cream, well chilled
1 teaspoon caster sugar
½ teaspoon vanilla bean paste
about 300g raspberries

1. Take two sheets of baking paper and, using the cookie cutter as a guide, draw around the inside of the cutter to make about 16 circles on each piece of baking paper. Try to keep the circles in neat lines, leaving about 2cm between each one. Turn the paper over so that the pencil lines are now on the underside – you should be able to see them through the paper – and place one on each baking sheet, ready for piping over.

2. Put the ground almonds and icing sugar in a food-processor and blend until the ingredients are ground to a fine powder. Lightly beat the egg whites with a fork, just enough to break them up. Weigh 50g of the egg white and add to the processor. Blend briefly to make a paste. Transfer to a bowl and put to one side.

3. Pour a 5cm depth of water into a medium pan and bring to a simmer. Put the remaining egg white in a large heatproof bowl that can rest over the pan of water without the bottom touching the water. Off the heat, **whisk** the egg whites until foamy. Add the caster sugar to the bowl and rest the pan over the hot water. Whisk with a hand-held electric whisk for about 3 minutes until the meringue forms **soft peaks** when the whisk is lifted from the bowl. Lift the bowl away from the heat and whisk for a further 3–4 minutes until the meringue is firm, thick and glossy.

4. Spoon 1 tablespoon of the meringue into a small bowl and add a little food colouring. The amount will vary depending on the brand so start with ¼ teaspoon, mixing it well until it's a deep, dark cerise. You might need to add a little more colouring.
Continued

5. Add the coloured paste to the almond mixture, and stir to blend. Stir in a quarter of the meringue mixture to loosen it up. Scrape this mixture out over the remaining meringue in the bowl. Using a large metal spoon **fold** the ingredients together gently until the mixture is no longer streaky. Avoid mixing any more than you need to or you'll lose the volume.

6. Fit the large piping bag with the plain piping nozzle and fill with the macaron mixture. **Pipe** rounds onto both pieces of the baking paper, using the circles as a guide. Stop filling each round when the mixture spreads to 5mm inside the edge of the circle. (It'll spread slightly more once you finish piping.) Leave the macarons to stand for 30 minutes until the surface is no longer sticky. Preheat the oven to 170°C (150°C fan), 325°F, Gas 3.

7. Bake the macarons for 10–12 minutes until the surfaces feel just crisp to the touch. Keep an eye on them for the last few minutes of baking in case they start to colour. Remove from the oven and leave to cool on the paper.

8. Put the 200ml whipping cream,
1 teaspoon caster sugar and
½ teaspoon vanilla bean paste in a
bowl and **whip** with a hand-held electric
whisk on a low speed until the cream
only just holds its shape.

9. Fit the cleaned piping bag with the
star nozzle and pipe swirls of cream
onto the bases of half the macarons.
Make sure the cream doesn't extend
beyond the edges of the macarons.
Arrange the 300g raspberries on top,
pointed ends uppermost. You'll need
about six raspberries for each. Position
the remaining macarons on top and
keep in a cool place until ready to serve.

Try Something Different

For lemon macarons, use lemon
yellow food colouring paste or gel to
colour the macarons. To assemble,
pipe the cream as above (omitting the
raspberries) and spread each macaron
lid with ½ teaspoon lemon curd
before gently pressing onto the cream.
Alternatively, try using orange food
colouring and orange curd.

Angel Cake with
Soft Fruits and
Coconut Cream

Angel cake is the lightest, airiest cake of all and one that takes a little practice to get just right, as it relies on careful folding of flour into a soft meringue. In this version, individual cakes are covered in a delicious coconut cream for a completely dairy-free treat.

Needs a little skill

HANDS-ON TIME:
40 minutes, plus several hours or overnight chilling, and cooling

BAKING TIME:
10–12 minutes

MAKES:
8 angel cakes

SPECIAL EQUIPMENT:
8 × 150ml metal pudding moulds, large baking sheet

STORAGE:
Keep the un-iced cakes for up to three days in an airtight container before finishing on the day of serving. These cakes also freeze well once finished with cream but before adding the fruits

vegetable oil, for brushing
65g plain flour, plus extra for dusting
75g icing sugar
6 medium egg whites, at room temperature
½ teaspoon cream of tartar
pinch of salt
75g caster sugar
1 teaspoon vanilla bean paste or extract

For the topping
2 x 160g tins coconut cream, chilled for several hours or overnight
2 tablespoons icing sugar
few drops of lemon juice
about 200g mixture of soft fruits e.g. raspberries, red- and blackcurrants and small strawberries

1. Position the oven shelf on the lowest rack and preheat the oven to 180°C (160°C fan), 350°F, Gas 4. Brush the metal pudding moulds with oil. Sprinkle a little flour into each and turn until the base and sides are evenly coated in flour. Tap out the excess. Sift together the flour and icing sugar and put to one side for now.

2. Put the egg whites into a large, spotlessly clean bowl with the cream of tartar and salt. Gently **whisk** using a hand-held electric whisk until frothy. (Alternatively use a free-standing electric mixer.) Increase the mixer speed and whisk until the mixture stands in soft, floppy peaks when the whisk is lifted from the bowl. At this point start to add the caster sugar, a tablespoonful at a time. Whisk well between each addition until the meringue is glossy and forms **soft peaks**. Add the vanilla with the last of the sugar.
Continued

3. Sift half the flour mixture into the bowl and **fold** in using a large metal spoon. Sift in the remaining flour mixture and fold in.

4. Divide the mixture among the moulds, spreading the mixture gently to keep in as much air as possible. Fill each tin so the top of the mixture is 1cm below the rim. Place on a baking sheet and bake for 10–12 minutes until slightly risen and springy to the touch. The crust should be pale, almost white, with the merest hint of colour in some areas.

5. Line a wire rack with baking paper to stop the cakes sticking. Loosen the edges of the cakes with the tip of a sharp knife and invert onto the paper leaving the metal moulds in place. If you try to remove the moulds while the cakes are still hot they're likely to collapse and lose their light airy texture. Once the cakes have cooled completely tap them out of the moulds onto the paper. If they refuse to budge, loosen the edges again, this time pushing the knife further down into the tins as the cake will have shrunk back slightly.

6. For the topping, scrape enough of the thick coconut cream that's set at the top of both 160g tins coconut cream into a bowl. As soon as you can get to the liquid underneath pour away 1 tablespoon from each tin (you won't need all of the liquid in the recipe). Scrape the rest of the coconut cream and the remaining liquid into the bowl and add the 2 tablespoons icing sugar and few drops of lemon juice. Whisk using a hand-held electric whisk, or a metal balloon whisk until the mixture is smooth and just holds its shape.

7. Spoon the cream onto the tops of the cakes and spread around the sides using a small palette knife until they're fairly smoothly coated. Arrange the 200g soft fruits on top to decorate. If the strawberries are large you might want to cut them in half first. Keep in a cool place until ready to serve.

Try Something Different

For alternative dairy-free flavourings for the angel cake omit the vanilla and add 1 piece of stem ginger from a jar, finely chopped, or ½ teaspoon ground ginger. Alternatively try adding the finely grated zest of 2 limes and pile banana sliced and steeped in lime juice on top instead of the soft fruits.

Chocolate Maple Tarts
with Hazelnut Brittle

Combine a hazelnut **pâte sucrée** with maple jelly and a creamy white and milk chocolate filling for the ultimate chocolate dessert, adorned with an impressive nut brittle decoration.

For the hazelnut pâte sucrée
25g hazelnuts
75g unsalted butter, at room temperature
2 tablespoons golden caster sugar
1 medium egg yolk
125g plain flour

For the filling
3 sheets leaf gelatine
150ml maple syrup
150g good-quality white chocolate, chopped
150ml double cream
150g good quality milk chocolate, chopped

For the hazelnut brittle
25g unblanched hazelnuts, toasted and chopped
100g caster sugar

HANDS-ON TIME:
1 hour, plus chilling and cooling

BAKING TIME:
20 minutes

MAKES:
6 tarts

SPECIAL EQUIPMENT:
6 individual 10cm round loose-bottomed plain or fluted tart tins, 2cm deep, baking sheet

METHOD USED:
Pâte sucrée, page 22

STORAGE:
Keep in a cool place for up to 24 hours before adding the brittle decoration to serve

1. First make the pastry. Heat a small, dry frying pan, add the nuts and heat for 4–5 minutes until the nuts are lightly toasted. Shake the pan frequently so they brown evenly. Leave to cool then blend in a food-processor until finely ground.

2. Put the butter and sugar in a bowl and cream together by beating with a wooden spoon until light and creamy. Beat in the egg yolk. Stir in the flour, about a third at a time. Add the cocoa powder and ground hazelnuts, then work the mixture together with your fingertips, along with 2 teaspoons of cold water (add a drop more if needed to bring the dough together), until it starts to clump together in big lumps and **form** a dough. Tip the dough onto the work surface and **knead** very briefly until smooth. Wrap in clingfilm and **chill** for 15 minutes in the freezer or 30 minutes in the fridge.

3. **Roll** out the pastry on a lightly floured surface to a 2mm thickness. **Cut out** six 13cm circles using a cutter or upturned bowl as a guide. Gather up the trimmings and re-roll them so you have enough pastry circles. Use to **line** the tins, easing the pastry into the corners and up the sides. Trim off the excess pastry around the tops. Prick the bases lightly with a fork and chill in the fridge for 15 minutes.

4. Preheat the oven to 200°C (180°C fan), 400°F, Gas 6 and put a baking sheet in the oven to heat up. Line the pastry cases with circles of baking paper and fill with baking beans or uncooked rice. Place the tins on the hot baking sheet and **blind bake** for 15 minutes. Remove the paper and beans and bake for a further 5 minutes, or until the pastry looks cooked. Leave to cool in the cases.
Continued

5. Next make the maple jelly for the filling. Put the 3 leaf gelatine sheets in a bowl of cold water and leave to soften for 5 minutes. Put 75ml of the maple syrup in a small pan and bring just to the boil. Lift the leaf gelatine sheets from the water. These will be floppy but still hold together. Let the excess water drip off and then, off the heat, lower the gelatine into the syrup. Shake the pan and you'll see the gelatine dissolve. Once completely dissolved, pour into a jug and add the remaining 75ml maple syrup. Chill in the fridge until thickened but not set.

6. Spoon the jelly into the tart cases and spread to the edges with the back of a teaspoon. Chill for at least 30 minutes until completely set.

7. To make the chocolate layers, put the 150g white chocolate and 75ml of the double cream in a small heatproof bowl and set over a pan of barely simmering water, making sure the bottom of the bowl doesn't touch the water. Heat for 1–2 minutes until the chocolate shows signs of melting. At this point turn off the heat but leave the bowl over the pan until the chocolate has melted, stirring the mixture occasionally.

8. Once the chocolate has melted, remove the bowl from the pan and leave to cool. At the point where it's thickened, but not setting, spoon it over the jelly and spread to the edges. Chill in the fridge while you prepare the 150g milk chocolate layer in the same way, using the remaining 75ml cream. Once cool, spoon into the tarts and spread level. Return to the fridge.

9. To make the hazelnut brittle, lightly oil a baking sheet. Scatter the 25g chopped hazelnuts onto the baking sheet in an even layer. Put the 100g caster sugar and 2 tablespoons water in a small pan and heat gently without stirring until the sugar dissolves and the **sugar syrup** is clear. This will take about 8–10 minutes. Once the syrup is completely clear bring it to the boil and boil for

about 5 minutes until the syrup turns to a golden amber colour. Immediately remove from the heat and drizzle the syrup in a fine stream over the nuts on the baking sheet. Leave for at least 30 minutes until completely brittle.

10. Break the brittle into shards and use to decorate the centres of the tarts. Transfer to serving plates.

Try Something Different

For a slightly less sweet version, use dark chocolate instead of the white chocolate. Omit the nut brittle and arrange a circle of roughly chopped toasted hazelnuts around the edges. Dust these lightly with cocoa powder.

Cinnamon Arlettes with Blackberry Jelly

Take home-made **puff pastry** one step further by adding a hint of cinnamon for a delicious culinary twist. The tangy blackberry jelly and vanilla cream makes a striking contrast in both appearance and flavour.

For the puff pastry
190g strong white bread flour
1½ teaspoons ground cinnamon
½ teaspoon salt
150g unsalted butter, chilled
1 teaspoon lemon juice
120ml cold water

For the blackberry jelly
250g blackberries
6 sheets leaf gelatine
125g caster sugar
2 teaspoons lemon juice

For the vanilla cream
300ml whipping cream, well chilled
4 tablespoons vanilla sugar, plus extra for dusting
200g blackberries, halved if large

HANDS-ON TIME:
1¼ hours, plus chilling and cooling

BAKING TIME:
25 minutes

MAKES:
12 arlettes

SPECIAL EQUIPMENT:
2 baking sheets, 20cm square cake tin, large 1cm plain piping nozzle, large piping bag

PASTRY USED:
Puff pastry, page 26

STORAGE:
Make the pastry and blackberry jelly a day ahead. Best baked and assembled on the day of serving

1. First make the pastry. Put the flour, cinnamon and salt in a large bowl. Take 15g of the butter and cut it into small dice. Add to the bowl and **rub** in with your fingertips to make a mixture that resembles fine breadcrumbs. Stir in the lemon juice and cold water. Mix with a round-bladed knife until the mixture comes together to **form** a fairly soft dough. Tip out onto a lightly floured surface and **knead** briefly for no more than a couple of minutes, just until you have a smooth dough. Wrap in clingfilm and **chill** for 30 minutes.

2. Put the remaining butter between two sheets of baking paper and flatten into a square block using a rolling pin. This needs to be 8mm thick and about 13cm across. If necessary, square up the shape with a palette knife. Leave wrapped in the baking paper and chill until needed.

Continued

3. **Roll** out the dough on a lightly floured surface until 20cm square. Brush off any excess flour. Peel off one sheet of paper from the butter and upturn the butter over the centre of the dough so the corners of the butter come halfway along (and slightly in from) the centre of the dough sides. Peel away the rest of the paper from the butter. Fold each corner of the dough up and over the butter to enclose it like an envelope. You should now have a square shape with no butter showing through. Turn the dough so a straight side faces you. Press the rolling pin over the dough several times to make indents and squash the butter slightly.

4. Roll the dough in light, short movements to a rectangle measuring about 40 x 15cm with a short side facing you. Fold the bottom third up over the centre third and the top third down so you have three layers. Seal the edges together by pressing down on them with the rolling pin. Give the dough a quarter turn and push a hole into the dough with your finger. This will remind you that you've rolled, layered and turned the dough once. (You'll repeat this process four more times and it's easy to forget how many have been done.) Wrap in a polythene food bag and chill for 20 minutes to firm up.

5. Repeat the rolling, folding and turning four more times, poking two holes in the dough the second time, three the third and so on, chilling the dough for 20 minutes each time. Chill the dough for at least 2 hours, or overnight, before use.

6. To make the blackberry jelly, run the square cake tin under the cold tap, tip out the excess water and line the tin with a sheet of clingfilm that comes up over the sides. Make sure the clingfilm fits right into the corners of the tin. Blend the 250g blackberries in a food-processor and scrape the purée out into a sieve set over a bowl. Press the pulp through the sieve with the back of a metal spoon to extract all the juice. Don't forget to include all the thick pulp on the underside of the sieve.

7. Fill a bowl with water and lower in the 6 gelatine sheets. Leave to soften in the water while you make the syrup.

8. Put the 125g caster sugar in a small pan with 40ml water and heat very gently until the sugar has dissolved and the syrup is clear. Remove from the heat. Lift out the gelatine sheets, which will now be soft and floppy, from the water. Once the water stops dripping off the gelatine, lower it into the hot syrup. Stir with a wooden spoon and pour the syrup into the blackberry purée, mixing well. Stir in the 2 teaspoons lemon juice and pour the mixture into the lined tin. Leave until cold then chill in the fridge for at least 4 hours or overnight to firm up.

9. Preheat the oven to 200°C (180°C fan), 400°F, Gas 6 and **line** the baking sheet with baking paper. Cut the pastry in half and roll out one half on a lightly floured surface to a 24cm square. Re-wrap the other half and chill in the fridge. Prick the base with a fork and place on the baking sheet. Chill for 15 minutes then trim off the uneven edges so you have a neat 22cm square.

10. Cover with a sheet of baking paper and position the second baking sheet on top. (This will stop the pastry rising too much as it bakes.) Bake for 10 minutes. Remove from the oven and prick the pastry once again with a fork. Return to the oven for a further 10 minutes. Remove the top baking sheet and paper and bake for a further 5 minutes until the pastry is evenly risen and golden. Slide off the baking sheet and leave to cool while you prepare the other half of the pastry in the same way.

Continued

11. Once cooled, cut each pastry square in half, then cut each half across into six even-sized rectangles (24 rectangles in all). Use a ruler as you do this to help you cut them precisely.

12. Lift the blackberry jelly out of the tin and place on a board, still in its clingfilm. Cut in half lengthways then cut each half across into 6 even-sized rectangles (12 rectangles in all). Chill in the fridge while you prepare the cream.

13. Put the 300ml chilled whipping cream and 4 tablespoons vanilla sugar in a bowl and **whip** using a hand-held electric whisk until it barely holds its shape. Transfer to the piping bag fitted with the plain nozzle. Select and reserve 12 well-shaped blackberries or blackberry halves from the 200g blackberries. Sprinkle the extra vanilla sugar onto a plate.

14. The arlettes are now ready to assemble. Lift the jelly pieces from the clingfilm and position them on half the pastry rectangles. **Pipe** two rows of cream down the length of each jelly. Arrange the blackberries over the cream, pressing them down gently, but not too far, into the cream. Dip the flat base of each of the remaining pastry rectangles in the vanilla sugar and position on top of the pastries, sugared sides face up. Finish each with one of the reserved blackberries in the centre.

Try Something Different

When whipping the cream and dusting the pastry rectangles, replace the vanilla sugar with regular caster sugar.

Mini Paris-Brest

Originally created to commemorate the Paris-Brest bike race, these lovely little cakes are as popular now as they ever were. As well as making **choux pastry**, this version uses home-made praline, another valuable patisserie skill.

For the choux pastry
100g plain flour
75g unsalted butter, diced
2 teaspoons caster sugar
pinch of salt
225ml water
3 medium eggs, beaten
5 tablespoons flaked almonds

For the crème patissière
3 medium egg yolks
25g caster sugar
25g cornflour
300ml milk
150ml double cream, well chilled

For the praline
75g whole blanched almonds
75g caster sugar
icing sugar, for dusting

1. Preheat the oven to 180°C (160°C fan), 350°F, Gas 4 and **line** two baking sheets with baking paper. Place the cutter on one sheet of paper and draw around it. Draw 11 more circles onto the paper, six on each sheet, spacing them at least 6cm apart. Turn the paper over.

2. Sift the flour onto a square of baking paper. This makes it easier to tip the flour quickly into the pan in one go. Put the butter into a medium pan with the sugar, salt and water. Heat gently until the butter has melted. Increase the heat until the liquid is at a rolling boil. Immediately tip in the flour and beat with a wooden spoon to make a thick paste.

3. With the pan still on the heat, beat the paste for 1–2 minutes until it is smooth and forms a ball that leaves the sides of the pan clean. Turn into a bowl and leave until the paste stops steaming, beating frequently.

4. Add a tablespoon of the beaten egg to the bowl and beat until absorbed before adding another spoonful. Continue beating in the egg until the dough is glossy and has a soft dropping consistency.
Continued

HANDS-ON TIME:
45 minutes, plus cooling

BAKING TIME:
35 minutes

MAKES:
12 Paris-Brest

SPECIAL EQUIPMENT:
3 baking sheets, 6cm round metal cutter, large star nozzle, large piping bag, large plain nozzle

PASTRY USED:
Choux pastry, page 28

STORAGE:
Serve on the day of baking, or keep the unfilled cakes in an airtight container for up to 2 days before filling and serving. If softened during storage, re-crisp in a moderate oven for 5–10 minutes, then cool and fill

5. Put the paste in the piping bag fitted with the star piping nozzle. **Pipe** the paste over the marked circles on the baking paper. Crumble the 5 tablespoons flaked almonds a little with your fingers and sprinkle over the pastry.

6. Bake for 30–35 minutes until the pastry is puffed and golden. Turn off the oven and leave the pastries inside with the door closed for 30 minutes. Transfer to a wire rack to cool completely.

7. To make the crème patissière, **whisk** together the 3 medium egg yolks, 25g caster sugar and 25g cornflour in a bowl until pale and creamy. Heat the 300ml milk in a pan until it just starts to come to the boil. Pour the hot milk over the egg yolks mixture, whisking well. As soon as the mixture is combined, pour it back into the pan. Cook over a low heat, stirring constantly with a wooden spoon until the sauce starts to thicken. You can then increase the heat a little to thicken the mixture, but keep stirring vigorously so it doesn't go lumpy. If it does, use a wire whisk, beating well until smooth again. Once the custard is very thick, scrape it into a clean bowl with a spatula and cover the surface with clingfilm to prevent a skin forming. Leave to cool.

8. To make the praline, oil a baking sheet ready for the **caramel**. Arrange the 75g almonds on the oiled sheet in an even layer. Put the 75g caster sugar in a small pan with the 1 tablespoon water and set over a low heat. Stir very occasionally with a wooden spoon until the sugar starts to melt and turn syrupy. This will take about 10 minutes. Increase

the heat to medium and cook until the syrup starts to colour, giving the pan a gentle shake from time to time. As soon as the syrup reaches a dark amber colour, pour it onto the nuts on the baking sheet, taking care as the mixture is very hot! Leave until cold and brittle. This will only take about 20 minutes.

9. Break the praline into pieces and put in a food-processor. Using the pulse setting, blend the praline until it is finely ground. Take care not to grind it to a paste – it still needs to be quite gritty. Stir the praline into the crème patissière.

10. Put the 150ml cream in a bowl and **whip** with a hand-held electric whisk on a low speed until the cream is only just beginning to hold its shape. Stir gently into the praline mixture.

11. Using a small, serrated knife, cut each of the pastry rings horizontally in half. Fit the plain piping nozzle into the cleaned piping bag and fill with the praline cream. Pipe a circle of the cream onto each pastry base and gently position the lids on top so the filling is visible. Dust lightly with icing sugar before serving.

Try Something Different

To make a large Paris-Brest, draw a 20cm circle onto a sheet of baking paper and invert onto a baking sheet. **Pipe** or spoon the choux pastry evenly over the marked circle. Scatter with almonds and bake as above, increasing the baking time by 5–10 minutes if necessary. Halve the choux ring horizontally and finish as above.

Cypriot Flaouna

These distinctively shaped breads show an interesting technique for enclosing a savoury filling within an enriched, yeasted dough. Mastic is ground from a tree gum and has a warm, almost pine-like flavour, while mahleb is a spice with a nutty, almond-like flavour. Both are available from online suppliers – although they give an authentic flavour, they're not essential to this dish.

Needs a little skill

HANDS-ON TIME:
1 hour, plus proving and overnight chilling

BAKING TIME
30 minutes

MAKES:
10 flaouna

SPECIAL EQUIPMENT:
2 baking sheets

STORAGE:
Best served freshly baked, or chill overnight and heat through in a moderate oven before serving

For the filling

60g semolina
50g plain flour
1 teaspoon dried mint
250g haloumi cheese, grated
200g Pecorino Romano or mature Cheddar, grated
50g sultanas
½ teaspoon salt
2 medium eggs, beaten
200ml milk
1 teaspoon baking powder

For the dough

400g strong white bread flour, plus extra for dusting
½ teaspoon salt
½ teaspoon mastic powder, or granules, ground to a powder using a pestle and mortar
1 teaspoon mahleb powder
20g fresh yeast
50g unsalted butter, melted
225ml milk

To finish

75g sesame seeds
2 teaspoons white wine vinegar
300ml water
2 egg yolks, to glaze

1. Make the filling the day before you prepare the pastry. Put the semolina, flour and dried mint in a bowl. Stir in both of the grated cheeses, the sultanas and the salt. Add the eggs and milk and stir all the ingredients together to combine. Cover with clingfilm and chill in the fridge overnight. (If you forget to make the filling a day in advance the recipe will still work well, although the filling will be slightly wetter.)
Continued

2. To make the dough, put the 400g strong white bread flour, ½ teaspoon salt, ½ teaspoon mastic powder and 1 teaspooon mahleb powder into a large bowl (or use the bowl of a free-standing mixer). Crumble in the 20g fresh yeast. Add the 50g melted unsalted butter and the 225ml milk and mix with a round-bladed knife until the mixture starts to come together to **form** a soft dough. Turn out onto a lightly floured surface and **knead** for 10 minutes until the dough is smooth and elastic. (Alternatively knead the dough for 6 minutes in the free-standing mixer, using the dough hook attachment.) Transfer the dough to a clean bowl, cover with clingfilm and leave to rise in a warm place for 1½–2 hours, or until the dough has doubled in size.

3. While the dough is rising, get everything else ready. **Line** the baking sheets with baking paper. Put the 75g sesame seeds in a small pan with the 2 teaspoons white wine vinegar and water. Bring the mixture to the boil then drain thoroughly through a sieve and turn the seeds out onto a clean tea towel. Spread in a thin layer. Beat the 1 teaspoon baking powder into the cheese filling. Beat the 2 egg yolks in a small bowl with 1 teaspoon water, ready for glazing.

4. Preheat the oven to 190°C (170°C fan), 375°F, Gas 5. Turn the dough out onto a lightly floured surface and divide into 10 even-sized pieces (each piece should weigh about 70g). **Roll** out one piece to a small circle measuring about 14cm in diameter. Lift onto the sesame seeds and press down lightly so the underside of the pastry becomes thickly coated in the seeds. Place to one side while you repeat with the remaining rounds.

5. Using a dessertspoon, divide the cheese filling among the centres of the round. Don't spread the filling over the dough – keep it in a fairly tight mound. To **shape** the pastry, bring three sides of one pastry circle up over the filling so you end up with a triangular shape. Pinch the dough edges together where

they meet to give a tricorn shape with the filling showing in the centre. Shape the remainder in the same way. Transfer five pastries to each baking sheet, spacing them well apart. Brush lightly with the egg yolks to **glaze**, using a dabbing action so you don't dislodge the sesame seeds.

6. Bake for 30 minutes until risen and golden. The filling should feel just set when lightly pressed with the fingers. Leave to cool for 15 minutes for serving warm or transfer to a wire rack to cool completely.

Almond Pithiviers
with Apricots

Making an elaborate French pithiviers is one of the most skilful ways of using home-made **puff pastry**. The addition of a tangy apricot layer counteracts the richness of the almond paste filling.

Needs a little skill

HANDS-ON TIME:
50 minutes, plus chilling and cooling

BAKING TIME:
35 minutes

MAKES:
8 servings

SPECIAL EQUIPMENT:
baking sheet, small metal piping nozzle

PASTRY USED:
Puff pastry, page 26

STORAGE:
Eat freshly baked or keep in an airtight container for up to 2 days. Best warmed through in a moderate oven for 10 minutes before serving

For the puff pastry
250g strong white bread flour
½ teaspoon salt
200g unsalted butter, chilled
2 teaspoons lemon juice
150ml cold water

For the filling
150g dried apricots, roughly chopped
4 tablespoons brandy or orange juice
3 tablespoons apricot jam
75g golden caster sugar
65g unsalted butter, softened
1 medium egg
75g ground almonds
½ teaspoon almond extract
beaten egg, to glaze
icing sugar, for dusting

1. Make the pastry first – this can be done a day in advance. Put the flour and salt in a large bowl. Take 15g of the butter and cut it into small dice. Add to the bowl and **rub in** with your fingertips to make a mixture that resembles fine breadcrumbs. Stir in the lemon juice and cold water. Mix with a round-bladed knife until the mixture comes together to **form** a fairly soft dough. Tip out onto a lightly floured surface and **knead** briefly for no more than a couple of minutes, just until you have a smooth dough. Wrap in clingfilm and **chill** for 30 minutes.

2. Put the remaining butter between two sheets of baking paper and flatten into a square block using a rolling pin. This needs to be a scant 1cm thick and about 16cm across. If necessary, square up the shape with a palette knife. Leave wrapped in the baking paper and chill until needed.

Continued.

3. **Roll** out the dough on a lightly floured surface until 23cm square. Brush off any excess flour. Peel off one sheet of paper from the butter and upturn the butter over the centre of the dough so the corners of the butter come halfway along (and slightly in from) the centre of the dough sides. Peel away the rest of the paper from the butter. Fold each corner of the dough up and over the butter to enclose it like an envelope. You should now have a square shape with no butter showing through.

4. Turn the dough so a straight side faces you. Press the rolling pin over the dough several times to make indents and squash the butter slightly.

5. For the second rolling, roll the dough in light, short movements to a rectangle measuring about 45 x 15cm with a short side facing you. Fold the bottom third up over the centre third and the top third down so you have three layers. Seal the edges together by pressing down on them with the rolling pin. Give the dough a quarter turn and push a hole in the dough with your finger. This will remind you that you've rolled, layered and turned the dough once. (You'll repeat this process four more times and it's easy to forget how many have been done.) Wrap in a polythene food bag and chill for 20 minutes to firm up.

6. Repeat the rolling, folding and turning four more times, poking two holes in the dough the second time, three the third and so on, chilling the dough for 20 minutes each time. Then chill the dough for at least 2 hours before use.

7. To make the apricot filling, put the 150g dried apricots in a small pan with the 4 tablespoons brandy or orange juice and 2 tablespoons water. Cook for about 5 minutes until almost all the liquid has evaporated. Stir in the 3 tablespoons jam and leave to cool.

8. To make the almond filling, put the 75g caster sugar, 65g butter, 1 egg, 75g ground almonds and ½ teaspoon almond extract in a bowl and beat with a hand-held electric whisk until pale and creamy. Scrape out onto a sheet of baking paper and using a small palette knife, form it into a neat drum shape, 12cm in diameter. Chill in the freezer for 10 minutes or in the fridge for 30 minutes. You're now ready to assemble the pithiviers.

Continued

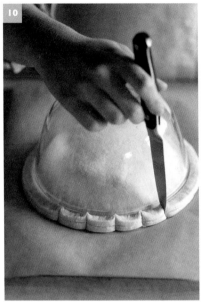

9. Preheat the oven to 220°C (200°C fan), 425°F, Gas 7 and **line** a baking sheet with baking paper. Roll out the dough on a lightly floured surface until it measures 43 x 22cm. Make sure you roll the dough in both directions so it's not over-stretched one way or other – the dough should be about 5mm thick. **Cut out** one 20cm round using an upturned bowl as a guide. Cut out another slightly larger 22cm round. Place the larger round on a tray lined with baking paper and chill while you finish making the base.

10. Transfer the smaller round to the lined baking sheet. Spoon the apricot mixture onto the pastry and level it out, leaving a generous 4cm border around the edges. Invert the almond 'drum' on top and peel away the paper. Brush the border

with beaten egg and carefully position the second pastry round on top. Fit it carefully over the filling, making sure you eliminate any pockets of air and easing the pastry to fit around the sides. The edges of both pastry layers should meet. Position a small bowl or tin with a diameter of 17cm over the pithiviers, pressing it down firmly into the pastry. Using the back of a small sharp knife, create a scalloped edge. Do this by holding the knife vertically and pushing the pastry from the edge up to the bowl or tin. Leave a 2cm space then repeat. Continue all around the base and carefully lift the container away.

11. Brush the top of the pastry with beaten egg to **glaze**, making sure you don't let any of the egg fall down the sides as it will prevent the pastry rising. Make a small hole in the top of the pie by pressing the thin end of the piping nozzle right through the pastry. Using the tip of the knife, make the traditional decoration: start at the hole in the centre of the pie and mark a shallow line with the tip of a sharp knife that curves out to the scalloped edge. Mark further shallow lines all around the pastry, making sure you don't cut more than 1mm through the pastry. Bake for 30 minutes or until risen and deep golden.

12. Remove from the oven and increase the temperature to 240°C (220°C fan), 475°F, Gas 9. Dust a fine layer of icing sugar all over the pithiviers, making sure it's evenly covered so you can no longer see the pastry. Return to the oven for several minutes. At this stage, don't move away from the oven. You'll need to check it after 2 minutes and then every minute until the icing sugar has melted to make a glossy, caramelly sheen. Serve freshly baked or at room temperature with pouring cream if liked.

Cheese and
Prosciutto
Croissants

Savoury croissants use the same basic dough as plain ones but are shaped and filled differently. Once you've mastered these, you'll find straightforward breakfast croissants even easier.

Needs a little skill

HANDS-ON TIME:
50–60 minutes, plus chilling

BAKING TIME:
17–20 minutes

MAKES:
16 croissants

SPECIAL EQUIPMENT:
2 large baking sheets

STORAGE:
Keep in an airtight container in a cool place for up to 24 hours. Warm through in a moderate oven before serving

For the croissant dough
400g strong white bread flour, plus extra for dusting
1 tablespoon caster sugar
½ teaspoon salt
20g fresh yeast
225ml milk
325g unsalted butter, chilled
beaten egg, to glaze

For the filling
16 slices prosciutto
200g raclette cheese, cut into 16 pieces

1. Put the flour, sugar and salt into a large bowl (or use the bowl of a free-standing mixer). Crumble in the yeast. Add the milk to the bowl and mix with a round-bladed knife until you have a soft dough. Dust your hands and the worktop generously with flour and **knead** the dough for 10 minutes until it feels smooth and elastic. (Alternatively knead the dough for 6 minutes in the free-standing mixer, using the dough hook attachment.) Place the dough in a clean bowl and **chill** in the fridge while you prepare the butter.

2. Put the block of butter between two sheets of baking paper and flatten into a rectangular slab by pushing it down firmly with a rolling pin until it measures 24 x 18cm. If necessary, tidy up the edges with a palette knife so the sides are fairly straight. Chill in the fridge, still in the paper, while you **roll** the dough.

3. Roll out the dough on a lightly floured surface to about 36 x 22cm. Invert the butter down onto the top two-thirds of the dough so that you have a 2cm border of dough around three sides of the butter and a large uncovered area at one end. Fold the uncovered end of the dough up over the middle third and then the upper third down so you end up with a three-layered rectangle.

4. Give the dough a quarter turn so a short end faces you. Press the rolling pin over the dough several times to make indents and squash the butter slightly.

5. For the next rolling, roll the dough in light, short movements to a rectangle measuring about 50 x 22cm. Fold the bottom third up over the centre third and the top third down so you have three layers. Seal the edges together by pressing down on them with the rolling pin. Give the dough a quarter turn clockwise and push a hole in the dough with your finger. This will remind you that you've rolled, layered and turned the dough once. Wrap in a polythene food bag and chill for 30 minutes to firm up.
Continued

6. Repeat the rolling, folding and turning three more times, poking two holes in the dough the second time, three the third and so on, chilling the dough for 20 minutes each time. Re-wrap the dough and chill for at least 4 hours or overnight. If you chill the dough overnight, it'll rise a little because of the yeast but will still be easy to roll and shape.

7. Preheat the oven to 200°C (180°C fan), 400°F, Gas 6 and **line** two baking sheets with baking paper. Cut the dough in half and return one half, wrapped, to the fridge. Roll out the remainder on a lightly floured surface to a 40 x 32cm rectangle. Cut in half widthways. Position the pieces with the short ends facing you. On one piece, make two nicks along the right hand long edge, one 8cm from one end and the other 8cm in from the other end. Make a nick along the left hand long edge, this time halfway along.

8. Using a large, sharp, floured knife make a cut through the dough from the lower left-hand corner to the first nick along the opposite edge. Then make a cut from this point to the nick halfway along the left-hand edge. Then make a cut from this point to the second nick on the right-hand edge, then finally back to the top left-hand corner. This will leave you with three triangles and two half-triangles. Press the two half triangles together along the long edges to make a fourth complete triangle. Do the same with the second rectangle and brush the edges with beaten egg.

9. Lay one of the 16 slices of prosciutto over each triangle so the edges extend over the edges of the triangle in places. This will ensure that the ham shows when the dough is rolled up. Position a piece of the 200g cheese at the thick ends of the triangles. Roll up each one, starting from the thick end. Transfer to a baking sheet, bending the thin ends round to resemble a classic croissant shape. Make sure the croissants are spaced well apart.

10. Repeat the whole process with the second batch of dough and the remaining prosciutto and cheese. Brush with beaten egg to **glaze** and leave to rise for 20 minutes before baking.

11. Bake for 17–20 minutes until risen and golden. (You might want to bake the first batch of croissants while you shape and fill the second batch.) Serve warm or soon after baking.

Try Something Different

For plain breakfast croissants, make and cut out the dough as above. Roll up the triangles without the filling and glaze and bake as above. You can also freeze the shaped croissants before baking: open-freeze until firm then wrap in plastic food bags. Take them out of the freezer the night before, place on a baking sheet lined with baking paper and cover loosely with a lightly floured tea towel. Bake as above.

Danish Pastries

These are made in a similar way to the croissants on page 138 but here the rich, yeasted dough is dotted with soft butter before layering and rolling. This recipe shows how to create the traditional 'windmill' shaping and has a delicious home-made marzipan and apricot flavouring. You can use canned apricots when fresh aren't in season.

HANDS-ON TIME:
1 hour, plus chilling

BAKING TIME:
15 minutes

MAKES:
18 pastries

SPECIAL
EQUIPMENT:
2 large baking sheets

STORAGE:
Best eaten freshly baked. Alternatively store, unglazed, for 2–3 days (or freeze for up to 3 months), and heat through in a moderate oven for 10 minutes before glazing and icing

For the Danish pastry dough
500g strong white bread flour, plus extra for dusting
3 tablespoons caster sugar
½ teaspoon salt
20g fresh yeast
2 medium eggs
225ml milk
225g unsalted butter, very soft
beaten egg, to glaze

For the marzipan
100g ground almonds
100g caster sugar
½ teaspoon almond extract
2 medium eggs

To finish
9 small apricots, halved and stoned
6 tablespoons apricot jam
100g icing sugar

1. Start by making the dough. Put the flour, sugar and salt into a large bowl (or use the bowl of a free-standing mixer). Crumble in the yeast and add the eggs. Add the milk to the bowl and mix with a round-bladed knife to **form** a soft dough. Dust your hands and the worktop generously with flour and **knead** the dough for 10 minutes until it feels smooth and elastic. (Alternatively knead the dough for 6 minutes in the free-standing mixer, using the dough hook attachment.) Place the dough in a clean bowl, cover with clingfilm and **chill** in the fridge for 1 hour.

2. Turn the dough out onto a floured surface and **roll** out until you have a rectangle measuring about 50 × 30cm. Dot the top two-thirds of the dough with the soft butter. This is easiest done with a small palette knife. Leave a 2cm border around the top and sides so the butter doesn't seep out during rolling. Bring the uncovered third of the dough up over the middle third, then fold the upper third over the middle to form a rectangle of three layers. Seal the edges together by pressing down on them with the rolling pin. Give the dough a quarter turn so a short end faces you. Press the rolling pin over the dough several times to make indents and squash the butter slightly. Wrap in a polythene food bag and chill for 30 minutes.
Continued

3. Position the block of dough on a lightly floured surface so a short end faces you. Roll out to a 60 × 30cm rectangle as before. Bring the lower third of the dough up to cover the middle third, then bring the remaining third down to make a rectangle as you did before. Seal the edges and give the dough a quarter turn. Repeat the rolling, folding, sealing and turning twice more. Wrap the dough in clingfilm and chill in the fridge for several hours or overnight, whichever suits you best. If you chill the dough overnight, it'll rise a little because of the yeast but will still be easy to roll and shape.

4. Before shaping the pastries make the marzipan by combining the 100g ground almonds, 100g caster sugar, ½ teaspoon almond extract and 2 eggs in a small bowl until you have a thick paste.

5. Preheat the oven to 200°C (180°C fan), 400°F, Gas 6 and **line** two baking sheets with baking paper. Cut the dough in half and return one half, wrapped, to the fridge. Roll out the other half on a lightly floured surface to a 32cm square. Trim off any ragged edges and cut the square into nine even-sized smaller squares. Using a small, sharp knife make a cut from one corner of a square, almost to the centre. Make three more cuts from the other corners almost to the centre. Bring one of the corner points over to the centre of the square (just beyond the end of the cut) and press down firmly. Repeat with the other three points so you end up with a windmill shape. Transfer to a baking sheet and repeat with the remaining eight squares.

6. Place a teaspoonful of the marzipan into the centre of each pastry, reserving half the paste for the second batch of dough. Press an apricot half, rounded side face up, over the marzipan. Brush with beaten egg to **glaze** and bake for 15 minutes until puffed and golden.

7. While the first batch is baking, shape and fill the second batch using the remaining dough, marzipan and apricots. (These can also be open-frozen on a baking sheet or tray, then wrapped in polythene food bags for another time.)

8. For the apricot glaze, press the 6 tablespoons apricot jam through a small sieve into a pan. Add 1 tablespoon water and heat through gently until thinned. Beat the 100g icing sugar in a bowl with 2 teaspoons water to make a smooth paste. The consistency needs to be smooth enough to drizzle with a teaspoon. You might need to add a few more drops of water but go cautiously as it's very easy to over-thin it.

9. Brush the apricot glaze all over the pastries. Transfer to a wire rack and drizzle with fine lines of icing.

Gateau St Honoré

This is another French patisserie classic that builds on the learned skills of making **choux pastry** and crème patissière. The main challenge is in its assembly – arranging choux buns on a **puff pastry** base, and holding it all together with a glossy, amber caramel.

Needs a little skill

HANDS-ON TIME:
1½ hours, plus cooling

BAKING TIME:
30 minutes

SERVES:
10

SPECIAL EQUIPMENT:
2 baking sheets, large piping bag, 1.5cm and 1cm plain round piping nozzles, St Honoré or large star nozzle

PASTRY USED:
Choux pastry, page 28

STORAGE:
Store the unfilled buns and base in an airtight container overnight. Assemble the gateau on the day of serving

For the base
200g bought or home-made puff pastry

For the choux pastry
65g plain flour
50g unsalted butter, diced
1 teaspoon caster sugar
pinch of salt
150ml water
2 medium eggs, beaten

For the crème patissière
1 vanilla pod
300ml milk
3 medium egg yolks
40g caster sugar
25g cornflour

To finish
200g caster sugar, plus 1 tablespoon
250ml whipping cream, well chilled
edible flowers, to decorate

1. Preheat the oven to 200°C (180°C fan), 400°F, Gas 6 and **line** two baking sheets with baking paper. To make the pastry base, first **roll** out the puff pastry on a lightly floured surface until large enough to **cut out** a 19cm circle, using a bowl or cake tin as a guide. Transfer to one baking sheet and prick with a fork. Chill while you prepare the choux pastry.

2. Sift the flour onto a square of baking paper. This makes it easier to tip the flour quickly into the pan in one go. Put the butter into a pan with the sugar, salt and water and heat gently until the butter has melted. Increase the heat until the liquid is at a rolling boil. Immediately tip in the flour and beat with a wooden spoon to make a thick paste.

3. With the pan still on the heat, beat the paste for 1–2 minutes until it is smooth and forms a ball that leaves the sides of the pan clean. Turn into a bowl and leave until the paste stops steaming, beating frequently.

4. Add a tablespoon of the beaten egg to the bowl and beat until absorbed before adding another spoonful. Continue beating in the egg, a tablespoon at a time, until the dough is glossy and has a soft dropping consistency.
Continued

5. Put the paste in the piping bag fitted with the larger plain nozzle. **Pipe** a border of choux pastry around the edge of the puff pastry circle. The outer edge of the choux pastry should just meet the edges of the puff pastry. Use the remaining choux pastry to pipe 14 small blobs, each about 3cm in diameter, onto the other baking sheet. If you have any more choux pastry mixture left in the bag, pipe an inner circle over the pastry base.

6. Bake the gateau base on the upper shelf of the oven and the small rounds on the lower shelf for 10 minutes. Reduce the oven temperature to 180°C (160°C fan), 350°F, Gas 4 and bake for a further 20 minutes until both pastries have risen and the choux is deep golden. Turn off the oven and leave the pastries for 30 minutes before transferring to a wire rack to cool completely.

7. To make the crème patissière, split the 1 vanilla pod lengthways with the tip of a knife and scrape the seeds into a pan with the 300ml milk – add the pod too. Heat over a low heat and remove from the heat as soon as it comes to the boil. Let the mixture sit for 15 minutes to infuse. **Whisk** together the 3 egg yolks, 40g caster sugar and 25g cornflour in a bowl with a wire whisk until smooth. Gradually pour half the vanilla-infused milk over the egg yolk mixture, whisking well as you do. The mixture will now be thinner so stir in the rest of the milk, including the vanilla pod.

8. Pour the mixture back into a clean pan. Cook over a low heat, stirring continuously with a wooden spoon for 10–12 minutes until thickened, adjusting the heat as you stir. Once the custard thickens slightly you can increase the heat a little. When it is very thick you can increase the heat further until bubbles rise up through the mixture. If the custard goes lumpy during the process you can remedy this by either beating it with a small wire whisk or pressing it through a sieve to make it smooth again. The custard should end up very thick, smooth and glossy. Remove the vanilla pod, transfer the custard to a clean bowl and cover the surface with clingfilm to prevent a skin forming. Leave until cold.

9. Spoon the cooled crème patissière into a clean piping bag fitted with the 1cm plain nozzle. Make a small slit on one side of each choux bun and pipe a little crème patissière into the centre. Pipe the remaining crème patissière over the pastry base and spread out evenly with a palette knife. Transfer the gateau to a serving plate.

Continued

10. Next make the **caramel**. For the next two steps you'll need to work quickly as caramel needs to be used before it starts to cool and set. Have ready a large bowl (or the washing up bowl), half-filled with cold water. Put the 200g caster sugar and 3 tablespoons water in a small pan and heat gently until the sugar dissolves and the syrup is clear. This will take about 10–15 minutes. Once the syrup is completely clear bring it to the boil and boil for about 5 minutes until the syrup turns to a golden amber colour. Immediately remove from the heat and dip the base of the pan briefly in the bowl of cold water.

11. Working quickly, dip the base of one of the little choux buns in the syrup and position it on the choux pastry ring around the sides of the pastry base. Dip another and place next to the first so they sit side by side. Continue to dip the buns in the syrup and secure around the edges of the base until filled. (You might have one or two buns over.) Lift the pan and carefully drizzle the remaining syrup over the tops of the buns so they're pleasingly covered and the syrup runs down the sides. If you find that the caramel has solidified before you've had a chance to cover the buns, you can heat it very gently to soften, but take care as it's very easy to burn the caramel at this stage.

12. Fit the St Honoré piping nozzle or star nozzle into a clean piping bag. **Whip** the 250ml cream in a bowl with the 1 tablespoon caster sugar until only just holding its shape. Spoon into the bag and pipe the cream in wavy lines over the crème patissière filling. Decorate with edible flowers to serve.

Savarin with
Clementines and Figs

Bathed in a sweet, mildly spiced fruit syrup, a yeasted savarin combines the skills of both bread-making and patisserie, and is well worth the extra bit of effort for a special occasion treat.

Needs a
little skill

For the savarin
250g strong white bread flour, plus extra for dusting
2 tablespoons caster sugar
¼ teaspoon salt
15g fresh yeast
100g unsalted butter
50ml milk
3 medium eggs, beaten

For the fruit syrup
4 small clementines
300g caster sugar
finely grated zest of 1 unwaxed lemon, plus 2 tablespoons juice
8g star anise
4 fresh figs
3 tablespoons apricot jam
2 tablespoons Grand Marnier or other orange-flavoured liqueur

For the chantilly cream
1 vanilla pod or 1 teaspoon vanilla bean paste
300ml whipping cream, well chilled
2 tablespoons icing sugar

HANDS-ON TIME:
1 hour, plus rising and cooling

HANDS-OFF TIME:
25 minutes

MAKES:
8 servings

SPECIAL EQUIPMENT:
ovenproof fluted ring tin or mould, about 20cm in diameter and 9cm deep, about 1.5 litre capacity

STORAGE:
Keep the baked but syrup free savarin in an airtight container for up to 2 days. Once bathed in syrup, keep in a cool place and serve within 24 hours, glazing just before serving

1. Thoroughly **grease** the fluted ring mould with melted butter. Sprinkle a little flour into the mould and tip the mould so the base and sides are coated in flour. Make sure you grease and flour the central column of the mould too. Tip out the excess flour and tap the mould gently to release any lumps of flour that might have collected.

2. Put the flour, sugar and salt into a large bowl (or use the bowl of a free-standing mixer). Crumble in the yeast. Dice the butter into a small pan and heat gently until melted, then remove from the heat. Stir the milk into the melted butter and check the temperature, which should feel neither hot nor cold to the touch. If it feels a bit hot, let it cool a little, then pour the mixture over the dry ingredients. Add the eggs and bring the dough together using a round-bladed knife. Use a wooden spoon (or the dough hook attachment of the mixer) to beat the batter until smooth and elastic. This will take about 5 minutes.

Continued

3. Scrape the batter out into the mould and spread with the back of a metal spoon so it's fairly level. (It'll level out a little more as it proves and bakes.) Leave to rise in a warm place, uncovered, for about 1¼–1½ hours, or until risen almost to the top of the mould. Towards the end of the rising time, preheat the oven to 200°C (180°C fan), 400°F, Gas 6.

4. Bake the savarin for 25 minutes, or until risen and firm to the touch. Leave in the mould for 15 minutes before loosening the edges with a knife and turning out onto a wire rack to cool.

5. While the savarin is cooling, make a start on the fruits and syrup. Peel the 4 small clementines, leaving them whole. Remove as much of the white, stringy pith as you can, then pierce all over with a metal skewer or tip of a small knife. Put the 300g caster sugar in a large pan with the zest of 1 lemon and 2 tablespoons juice, 8g star anise and 500ml water. Heat gently until the sugar dissolves. Add the clementines and 4 figs and cook on the lowest possible heat for 10 minutes, just to soften. Drain with a slotted spoon and leave the syrup to cool until lukewarm.

6. If the savarin has risen slightly unevenly and tilts to one side, slice a little off the base (it won't need much), to level it up.

7. Place the savarin in a large bowl and pour the syrup over it. Turn the savarin in the syrup and lift out onto a lipped plate. Ladle the syrup over the top and into the centre of the savarin. The aim is to make the savarin as syrupy and juicy as you can. When the plate fills up, pour the syrup back into the bowl and start spooning again. Once you have about 150ml unabsorbed syrup left, pour this into a small pan and transfer the savarin to a serving plate. Take care here as it'll be softer than it was before steeping.

8. Bring the syrup to the boil. Boil for 3 minutes to thicken slightly then remove from the heat. Press the 3 tablespoons apricot jam through a small sieve into the syrup. Stir in the 2 tablespoons liqueur.

9. For the chantilly cream, split the vanilla pod lengthways and scrape out the seeds with the tip of a small knife. Place these in a bowl and add the 300ml cream and 2 tablespoons icing sugar. **Whip** with a hand-held electric whisk until **soft peaks** form. Transfer to a serving bowl.

10. Halve the clementines and figs and pack into the centre of the savarin, arranging the prettier pieces on top. Just before serving, spoon the boozy syrup all over the fruits and down the sides of the cake so it's generously coated. Serve with the chantilly cream.

Chocolate
Mont Blanc
Cups

Making chocolate cases is one of the more advanced patisserie skills. Set around a moist chocolate sponge and piled up with a classic 'Mont Blanc' topping, these delicate chocolate cups make a stunning dinner party dessert or celebration tea.

Up for a challenge

HANDS-ON TIME:
1¼ hours, plus chilling and cooling

BAKING TIME:
15 minutes

MAKES:
6 cups

SPECIAL EQUIPMENT:
20cm square shallow baking tin, 2 baking sheets, 6 × 7cm metal baking rings, 36 × 25cm sheet of acetate, disposable piping bag, 6cm round pastry cutter, small piping bag, large writer nozzle

STORAGE:
Keep for up to 24 hours in a very cool place or in the fridge

For the sponge
90g good-quality dark chocolate, preferably a minimum of 70 per cent cocoa solids, chopped
3 medium eggs, at room temperature
pinch of salt
90g golden caster sugar

For the chocolate cases and decoration
250g good-quality dark chocolate, preferably a minimum of 70 per cent cocoa solids, chopped
edible gold leaf (optional)

For the filling
200g unsweetened chestnut purée
50g golden caster sugar
150ml double cream, well chilled
1 tablespoon dark rum or brandy (optional)

To make the sponge

1. Preheat the oven to 180°C (160°C fan), 350°F, Gas 4 and **grease and line** the square tin with baking paper. Grease the paper as well.

2. Put the dark chocolate into a heatproof bowl and set over a pan of gently simmering water, making sure the bottom of the bowl doesn't touch the water. Leave until the chocolate has melted, stirring now and again. Remove the bowl from the pan, stir until smooth and leave until needed.

3. Separate the eggs, putting the whites in one large, thoroughly clean bowl and the yolks into another large bowl.

4. Add the salt to the egg whites and **whisk** using a hand-held electric whisk until the whites stand in **soft peaks** when the whisk is lifted. Put to one side while you prepare the yolks.

5. Add the sugar to the egg yolks. Take the whisk (there's no need to clean it first) and whisk for about 3 minutes until the mixture is very thick and leaves a distinct ribbon-like trail when the whisk is lifted. Pour the cooled melted chocolate into the bowl and gently **fold** in with a plastic spatula or large metal spoon.
Continued

6. Add a third of the whisked egg whites to the bowl and stir in to loosen the mixture then gently fold in the rest of the whites using the spatula or spoon. Scrape the mixture into the prepared tin and gently ease it into the corners so that the mixture is level. Bake for 15 minutes, or until risen. The cake should feel just firm when lightly pressed with a finger. Carefully lift the sponge out of the tin and onto a wire rack. Don't worry if the surface of the cake sinks slightly.

To make the chocolate cases and decoration

7. While the sponge is cooling, make the chocolate cases. Line a baking sheet with baking paper and position the metal baking rings on the paper. Cut the acetate sheet widthways into six strips, each measuring 25 x 6cm. Take care with the cutting as perfectly straight lines are needed. Roll each strip and fit inside a baking ring. Secure the overlapping ends on the outside with tape to stop the acetate springing open when the rings are removed.

8. Melt 200g of the chocolate for the cases as you did in Step 2. Spoon two dessertspoonsful onto the baking paper inside one metal ring. Holding the ring in place with one hand, brush the chocolate up the acetate with a thoroughly clean pastry brush. Use vertical movements with the brush and stop just short of the top of the acetate. The cups look particularly effective when the chocolate around the top edge is irregular so don't worry too much about neatness. Just make sure the chocolate is of even thickness so there are no weak areas that might break when the cases are unmoulded. Fill the remaining cases in the same way. Leave the cases in a cool place for several hours until the chocolate is brittle. If the weather is warm you might need to chill the cases in the fridge for 30 minutes to firm up.

9. To finish the cases, lift them away from the paper and carefully remove the metal rings. Peel away the tape and then the acetate. Return the cases to a cool place (or the fridge).

Continued

10. Draw six 7cm circles onto a sheet of baking paper using one of the baking rings as a guide. Invert onto another baking sheet. Melt the remaining 50g chocolate as in Step 2 and transfer to a disposable piping bag. Snip off the smallest tip you can cut so the chocolate can be piped in a fine line. You can snip a little more off if the line is too fine but avoid snipping off too much. **Pipe** squiggly lines of chocolate into the marked circles on the paper. This is much easier to do than it sounds, as you don't have to worry about straight lines or precision. It doesn't matter if the piping goes over the edge either – the marked circles are merely a guide. Stop piping before the circles become too densely filled with chocolate. At this point, add the gold leaf decoration if you're using it. To do this, tear small pieces of gold leaf from its paper using the tips of two sharp knives. (Gold leaf is almost weightless and will quiver and move as you lift it.) Position a small piece on the centre of each chocolate decoration. Chill in the fridge while you prepare the filling.

To make the filling

11. Peel the paper away from the chocolate sponge. **Cut out** six circles of sponge using the 6cm pastry cutter. Lift away the cake trimmings and freeze these for a chocolate trifle (or eat with tea or coffee!).

12. Put the 200g chestnut purée, 50g golden caster sugar, 150ml double cream and 1 tablespoon rum or brandy (if using) in a medium bowl and whisk with a hand-held electric whisk or a balloon whisk until smoothly combined. Continue to whisk for a few minutes until the mixture starts to thicken and hold its shape.

To assemble the cups

13. Place a dessertspoonful of the filling into each of the chocolate cases. Lift a circle of sponge by piercing the top with a fork and lower into each case so it rests over the cream. Spoon a further dessertspoonful of the chestnut mixture on top and spread to the edges.

14. Put the remaining chestnut mixture in a small piping bag fitted with the writer nozzle. Use to pipe squiggly lines of the chestnut mixture into each cup. Pipe it evenly over the surface to start with and then pile it up a little in the centre to give it height.

15. Carefully peel the paper away from the chocolate decorations and position over the filling. Arrange each decoration vertically so you push it down into the filling slightly for support, or flat so it rests on the chocolate case. Chill until ready to serve.

Cardamom
and Orange
Baklava

This recipe shows how achievable home-made **filo pastry** really is. Here it's used with traditional Baklava ingredients but served as a round gateau with candied orange decoration.

Up for a challenge

HANDS-ON TIME:
1¼–1½ hours, plus
resting and cooling

BAKING TIME:
1 hour

MAKES:
12 slices

SPECIAL
EQUIPMENT:
23cm round
springclip tin, large
lipped baking sheet
or heatproof tray,
small baking sheet

METHOD USED:
Filo pastry, page 27

STORAGE:
Keep for up to
3 days in an airtight
container in a cool
place

For the the filo pastry
325g plain flour, plus extra for dusting
½ teaspoon salt
150ml warm milk
1 teaspoon red or white wine vinegar
75g unsalted butter, melted

For the filling
200g blanched almonds
100g cashew nuts
100g walnut pieces
50g golden caster sugar
seeds from 20 cardamom pods,
crushed, or 1 teaspoon ground
cardamom
finely grated zest of 1 unwaxed orange

For the syrup
200g golden caster sugar
1 tablespoon lemon juice
6 tablespoons clear honey
2 teaspoons orange blossom water
juice of ½ orange

To assemble
100g unsalted butter, melted
4 tablespoons cornflour
finely pared zest of 2 unwaxed
oranges, with no white pith
50g caster sugar
¼ teaspoon ground cinnamon
icing sugar, for dusting

To make the filo pastry
1. Put the flour, salt, milk, vinegar and butter in a large bowl (or use the bowl of a free-standing mixer) and mix with a round-bladed knife until it comes together to **form** a soft dough. Dust your hands and the work surface generously with flour, tip the dough out and **knead** for 10 minutes until smooth and silky. (Alternatively knead the dough for 5 minutes in the free-standing mixer.) Transfer to a clean bowl, cover and leave in a cool place for 30 minutes.

To make the filling
2. In the meantime, put all the nuts in a food-processor and pulse. Stop when some of the nuts are finely chopped and others are slightly chunkier. Tip into a bowl and stir in the sugar, cardamom and orange zest. Put to one side.

To make the syrup
3. Very gently heat the sugar, lemon juice and 100ml water in a small pan until the sugar has dissolved, stirring once or twice. Once the **sugar syrup** is completely clear, bring to the boil and boil for 5 minutes. Remove from the heat, stir in the honey, orange blossom water and orange juice. Leave to cool.

To assemble the baklava
4. Use a little of the 100g melted butter to brush the base and sides of the 23cm springclip tin. Put the dough on a generously floured surface and cut into quarters. Cut one quarter into four pieces. **Roll** one of the pieces to a rough circle about 15cm in diameter. Repeat with the other three small pieces (work with just one quarter at a time, to stop the dough drying out).
Continued

5. Spoon I teaspoon of cornflour onto each of three of the rounds and spread with your fingers in an even layer. Stack the three cornfloured rounds together and position the uncornfloured round on top. Roll the four layers together until you have a circle about 26cm in diameter. Keep rotating the pastry as you go to keep the circle as neat as possible.

6. Peel away one of the four layers (the cornflour will keep the layers separate) and position in the base of the tin. Brush with a little melted butter. Peel away another of the pastry layers and arrange over the first in the tin. Brush with more butter. Repeat with the remaining two layers, brushing each with butter. The layers needn't meet the edges of the tin perfectly and it doesn't matter if there are creases – just make sure the tin gets filled with an even layering of pastry.

7. Preheat the oven to 180°C (160°C fan), 350°F, Gas 4. Sprinkle a third of the nut mixture into the tin and spread to the edges. Take another quarter of the dough and repeat the process of cutting, rolling, layering with cornflour and thinly rolling the stack. Layer up over the nuts, brushing each layer with more butter. Cover with half the remaining nuts. Use another quarter of the dough to fill the tin with four more layers, then add the remaining nuts and finally four more layers of filo. Use a sharp knife to deeply score the top layer of dough with neat lines, about 3cm apart.

8. Bake for 1 hour until the pastry is crisp and golden. Place the tin on the baking tray or heatproof tray and pour the syrup all over the surface. Leave for at least 2 hours or overnight, until the syrup has been absorbed into the layers.

To decorate

9. Preheat the grill to moderate. **Line** a small baking sheet with baking paper. Slice the pieces of finely pared zest from 2 oranges as thinly as you can with a sharp knife. Combine the zest with the 50g caster sugar and ¼ teaspoon ground cinnamon and tip out onto the paper. Spread the mixture out in a thin layer. Place under the grill for about 3 minutes until the sugar is just starting to turn to a syrup in patches but is still quite white and crunchy. Watch closely as the sugar will turn quite quickly.

10. Once the orange sugar is cool enough to handle, use your fingers to scrunch it into small pieces. Lift the baklava out of the tin and transfer to a serving plate. Sprinkle the orange sugar along alternate grooves over the surface of the cake. Sprinkle fine lines of icing sugar along the remaining lines, using a spoon. Serve cut into small wedges.

Try Something Different

For a delicate rose flavour, use 1 teaspoon rosewater in the syrup instead of the orange blossom water. **Roll** out the dough to roughly 23cm squares instead of rounds and layer up in a 20cm square loose-bottomed tin. Serve cut into small squares.

The success of a millefeuilles relies on the making and accurate shaping of **puff pastry**. Layered up with fresh raspberries and crème diplomat (a cream-enriched crème patissière), this stunning creation showcases a feast of patisserie skills.

Up for a challenge

For the puff pastry
190g strong white bread flour, plus extra for dusting
½ teaspoon salt
150g firm, unsalted butter
1 teaspoon lemon juice
110ml cold water

For the crème diplomat
1 vanilla pod
300ml milk
3 medium egg yolks
65g caster sugar
25g cornflour
150ml double cream, well chilled

To finish
400g raspberries
2–3 tablespoons freeze-dried raspberry powder
icing sugar, for dusting

HANDS-ON TIME:
1¼ hours, plus chilling and cooling

BAKING TIME:
25 minutes

MAKES:
8 slices

SPECIAL EQUIPMENT:
2 baking sheets, large piping bag, large star nozzle

METHOD USED:
Puff pastry, page 26

STORAGE:
Make the pastry and crème diplomat a day ahead. Best baked and assembled on the day of serving

To make the puff pastry
1. Put the flour and salt in a large bowl. Take 15g of the butter and cut it into small dice. Add to the bowl and **rub in** with your fingertips to make a mixture that resembles fine breadcrumbs. Stir in the lemon juice and cold water. Mix with a round-bladed knife until the mixture comes together to make a fairly soft dough. Tip out onto a lightly floured surface and **knead** briefly for no more than a couple of minutes, just until you have a smooth dough. Wrap in clingfilm and **chill** for 30 minutes.

2. Put the remaining butter between two sheets of baking paper and use a rolling pin to flatten into a 13cm square, about 8mm thick. If necessary, square up the shape with a palette knife. Leave wrapped in the baking paper and chill until needed.

3. **Roll** out the dough on a lightly floured surface to a 21cm square. Brush off any excess flour. Peel off one sheet of paper from the butter and upturn the butter over the centre of the dough so the corners of the butter come halfway along (and slightly in from) the centre of the dough sides. Peel away the paper from the butter. Fold each corner of the dough up and over the butter to enclose it like an envelope. You should now have a square shape with no butter showing through. Turn the dough so a straight side faces you. Press the rolling pin over the dough several times to make indents and squash the butter slightly.
Continued

4. Roll the dough in light, short movements to a rectangle measuring about 40 x 16cm with a short side facing you. Fold the bottom third up over the centre third and the top third down so you have three layers. Seal the edges together by pressing down on them with the rolling pin. Give the dough a quarter turn and push a hole in the dough with your finger. This will remind you that you've rolled, layered and turned the dough once. Wrap in a polythene food bag and chill for 20 minutes to firm up.

5. Repeat the rolling, folding and turning four more times, poking two holes in the dough the second time, three the third and so on, chilling the dough for 20 minutes each time. Chill the dough for at least 2 hours before use.

To make the crème diplomat
6. Use the tip of a knife to scrape the seeds from the 1 vanilla pod into a pan with the 300ml milk — add the pod as well. Place over a low heat just until it comes to the boil, then remove from the heat and let the mixture infuse and cool for 15 minutes.

7. **Whisk** together the 3 egg yolks, 40g of the caster sugar and the 25g cornflour in a bowl with a wire whisk until smooth. Gradually pour half the vanilla-infused milk over the egg yolk mixture, whisking well. The mixture will now be thinner so stir in the rest of the milk, including the vanilla pod.

8. Pour back into a clean pan. Cook over a low heat, stirring continuously with a wooden spoon for 10–12 minutes until

thickened – once the custard thickens slightly you can increase the heat a little. Once very thick you can increase the heat further until bubbles rise up through the mixture. If the custard goes lumpy during the process you can remedy this by either beating it with a small wire whisk or pressing it through a sieve to make it smooth again. The custard should end up very thick, smooth and glossy. Transfer the custard to a clean bowl, remove the vanilla pod and cover the surface with clingfilm to prevent a skin forming. Leave until cold.

To bake the pastry

9. Preheat the oven to 220°C (200°C fan), 425°F, Gas 7 and **line** a baking sheet with baking paper. Roll out the dough on a lightly floured surface until it measures 40 x 33cm. Try to keep the edges neat and straight as you roll by always rolling up and down, or across the dough rather than diagonally. Trim off the uneven edges with a large, sharp knife and transfer to the baking sheet. Prick the pastry all over with a fork and pop it in the freezer for 10 minutes or the fridge for 20 minutes.

10. Dust the pastry all over with icing sugar. Cover with a sheet of baking paper and position the second baking sheet on top (this will stop the pastry rising too much as it bakes). Bake for 10 minutes. Remove from the oven and prick the pastry once again with a fork. Cover with the baking paper and baking sheet again and return to the oven for a further 10 minutes. Remove the baking sheet and paper and bake for a further 5 minutes, until the pastry is evenly risen and golden. Leave to cool on the baking sheet.

Continued

11. Using a serrated knife, cut off the edges of the pastry to neaten. Use a ruler as you do this to make sure that the length and width of the rectangle remain the same. Cut the pastry widthways into three, even-sized rectangles.

To assemble the millefeuilles

12. To finish the crème diplomat put the 150ml double cream and remaining 25g sugar in a bowl and **whip** until the cream forms **soft peaks** when the whisk is lifted from the bowl. Scrape the cream into the crème patissière and stir gently together with a large metal spoon until combined.

13. Fit the piping nozzle into the piping bag and fill with the cream. **Pipe** swirls down the centre of two of the pastry rectangles. Pipe further swirls down the edges of the pastries so the outer edges of the cream swirls are in line with the edges of the pastry.

14. Take the 400g raspberries and reserve 8–10 of the best ones for decorating. Arrange four rows of the remaining raspberries, pointed ends up, over the cream. The raspberries in the rows should be touching, but with a small gap in between the rows. Dust the raspberries lightly with icing sugar. Carefully transfer one of the topped pastry rectangles to a serving plate and position the other topped pastry rectangle on top.

15. Turn the remaining pastry rectangle over so the flat side faces up and dust this generously with icing sugar. Sprinkle the 2–3 tablespoons freeze-dried raspberry powder in a thick line down the centre of the pastry with your fingers. Position on top of the other layers and arrange the reserved raspberries down the centre. Use a large, sharp knife to cut into slices.

Nectarine and Amaretti Gateau

Crushed amaretti biscuits flavour this **whisked sponge** recipe, giving a really nutty flavour and contrast to the layers of almond chantilly and fresh, juicy nectarines. Its crowning glory (though optional) is a nest of spun sugar!

For the sponge
100g amaretti biscuits
4 medium eggs, at room temperature
75g golden caster sugar, plus extra for dusting
75g plain flour
pinch of salt
50g unsalted butter, melted

For the filling
4 large fresh nectarines

juice of ½ lemon
300ml double cream, well chilled
2 tablespoons icing sugar
2 tablespoons amaretto liqueur

For the almond coating
100g flaked almonds

For the spun sugar
200g caster sugar
75ml water

Up for a challenge

HANDS-ON TIME:
1¼–1½ hours,
plus cooling

BAKING TIME:
20–25 minutes

MAKES:
12 slices

SPECIAL
EQUIPMENT:
2 × 18cm square
shallow cake tins,
large baking sheet

METHOD USED:
Whisked sponge,
page 29

STORAGE:
Keep in an airtight
container, preferably
in a cool place, or
the fridge overnight.
Decorate with spun
sugar on the day of
serving

To make the sponge

1. Preheat the oven to 180°C (160°C fan), 350°F, Gas 4. **Grease and line** the bases of two 18cm sandwich tins with baking paper. Put the amaretti biscuits in a food bag and crush with a rolling pin until finely ground.

2. Put the eggs and sugar in a large bowl and **whisk** with a hand-held electric whisk, or in a free-standing mixer for 6–8 minutes until pale. You should end up with a thick, foamy mixture and the whisk should leave a thick, ribbon-like trail when lifted.

3. Sift the flour and salt into a bowl, then sift it again over the egg mixture and sprinkle with the crushed biscuits. Gently **fold** in the dry ingredients until no lumps remain, taking care not to knock out the air you've whisked in. Once evenly combined drizzle the melted butter all over the surface and fold in very gently. Divide between the prepared tins and spread level.

4. Bake for 20–25 minutes until risen, pale golden and just firm when gently pressed in the centre. Run a knife around the inside of the tins to loosen the sponges. Cover a wire rack with a sheet of baking paper and sprinkle with a little caster sugar. Turn out the sponges onto the paper and leave to cool completely. At this stage the sponges can be left overnight to firm up before decorating. If serving on the same day, pop the cooled cakes in the freezer for 30 minutes. Dry-fry the 100g flaked almonds for the coating in a frying pan for 2–3 minutes, turning frequently until lightly toasted. Tip onto a sheet of baking paper to cool.

To make the filling

5. Halve the 4 nectarines and very thinly slice. You need 2 nectarines evenly sliced for the decoration but you needn't take such care with the 2 for the filling. Spread the slices out on a plate and squeeze the juice of ½ lemon over the top. Have a flat serving plate ready.
Continued

6. To make the almond chantilly, put the 300ml double cream, 2 tablespoons icing sugar and 2 tablespoons amaretto liqueur in a bowl and **whip** with a hand-held electric whisk until **soft peaks** form. Beat the cream a little more with a wooden spoon until the peaks hold their shape a little more firmly. Take care not to over-beat the cream or it'll become dry and the texture grainy.

To assemble the cake

7. Using a palette knife, spread a quarter of the cream over one of the cake layers, set on a sheet of baking paper. Arrange the nectarines for the filling over the top in an even layer. Spread a further quarter of the cream on top of the nectarines and invert the second cake on top so the base is uppermost. Spread most of the remaining cream around the sides of the cake, filling any gaps and making the corners as neat as possible.

8. To coat the sides in almonds, first slide the gateau to the edge of the work surface so you can slide the palm of one hand underneath the paper to support it. Position the other palm on top of the cake and flip the cake over so you can peel away the base paper. Carefully turn the cake so you're holding it vertically and rest gently in the flaked almonds. Twist the cake between your palms so you can coat the other sides in the same way. Once you've coated two or three sides you might need to flip the cake horizontally onto one palm again while you re-arrange the almonds that might have scattered.

9. Transfer the gateau to the serving plate you have ready. Spread the remaining cream over the top in a thin layer. Arrange the remaining nectarine slices in three neat rows over the surface. Keep in a cool place, or the fridge, while you prepare the spun sugar.

To make the spun sugar
10. Line the baking sheet with baking paper. Put the 200g caster sugar in a small heavy-based pan with 75ml water. Cook on the lowest heat possible to dissolve the sugar. Avoid stirring or you risk crystallising the syrup. When the sugar has dissolved increase the heat and clip a sugar thermometer to the side of the pan. Cook the syrup, watching closely, until it starts to turn pale golden and reaches 155°C (310°F). Remove from the heat and leave for 3 minutes while you lightly oil a rolling pin.

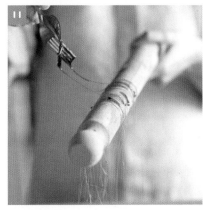

11. Holding the rolling pin in one hand, and two forks (held face to face) in the other, dip the forks in the caramel, lift up a little syrup and flick the forks back and forth across the rolling pin so the caramel turns to fine, brittle strands. Working quickly, snap the set strands onto the baking paper and repeat the process of lifting and flicking the syrup until you end up with a nest of sugar strands on the baking sheet. Gather up the strands and lift onto the gateau, leaving them in a pile in the centre or spreading them out into the corners.

This impressive gateau uses the 'Jaconde' technique in which contrasting flavours of sponge are piped to create a stunning sponge case. It's filled with a rich chocolate mousse, pistachio topping and delicately moulded chocolate flowers.

For the 'biscuit' sponge
40g unsalted butter
4 medium eggs, at room temperature
pinch of salt
100g caster sugar
100g plain flour
2 tablespoons cocoa powder

For the chocolate mousse
250g good-quality dark chocolate,
preferably a minimum of 70 per cent
cocoa solids, chopped
7 tablespoons double cream
5 medium egg whites, at room
temperature
50g caster sugar

For the pistachio cream
200g unsalted, shelled pistachio nuts
100g icing sugar
75g unsalted butter, softened

For the decoration
150g dark chocolate modelling paste

HANDS-ON TIME:
1½–1¾ hours, plus
cooling and chilling

BAKING TIME:
17–20 minutes

MAKES:
12 servings

**SPECIAL
EQUIPMENT:**
30 × 20cm Swiss
roll tin, 18cm round
springclip tin, 2 large
piping bags and
2 × 1cm plain piping
nozzles

METHOD USED:
Whisked sponge,
page 29

STORAGE:
Keep for up to 2 days
in a cool place

To prepare the pistachio cream
1. Put the pistachio nuts in a heatproof bowl and just cover with boiling water. Leave to stand for 1 minute then drain through a sieve and tip out onto a clean kitchen cloth. Bring up the sides of the cloth so the nuts are contained and rub between your hands for a couple of minutes. This will help to remove the brown skins. Open out the cloth and transfer all the nuts that have peeled into a food-processor. Some of the skins will stick stubbornly and these are best peeled away with your fingers. You needn't be too thorough with this but the more skins you remove, the better the colour of the pistachio cream. Blend the nuts until ground as finely as possible. Measure 25g into a small bowl.

To make the 'biscuit' sponge
2. Preheat the oven to 180°C (160°C fan), 350°F, Gas 4. **Grease** the Swiss roll tin and the 18cm round springclip tin with butter. **Line** with baking paper and grease the paper. Melt the butter and leave to cool.

3. Separate the eggs, putting the whites into a large, spotlessly clean, grease-free bowl. Put the egg yolks into a separate, large bowl. Add a pinch of salt to the whites and **whisk** with a hand-held electric whisk until **soft peaks** form. Gradually whisk in half the sugar, a couple of tablespoonfuls at a time, to make a light meringue. Put the bowl to one side while you prepare the yolks. *Continued*

4. Add the remaining 50g sugar to the yolks. Take the whisk (there's no need to clean it first) and whisk for 3–5 minutes until the mixture becomes very light, thickened and mousse-like. It should fall in thick ribbons when the whisk is lifted from the bowl. Add a third of the meringue to the bowl and **fold** in using a large metal spoon or plastic spatula. Add the remaining meringue to the bowl and fold in. Sift the 100g plain flour into the bowl and once again fold in until the ingredients are just combined. Drizzle the cooled butter over the surface of the bowl and carefully fold in as before.

5. Transfer 100g of the mixture to the round cake tin. This is easiest done by putting the tin on digital scales and pouring in the sponge mixture. Ease the mixture gently to the edges of the tin. Transfer another 125g of the mixture to a separate bowl and fold in the 25g ground pistachio nuts. Sift the 2 tablespoons cocoa powder into the remaining mixture and fold in. Transfer the mixtures to the piping bags, each fitted with a plain nozzle. Take the bag containing the pistachio mixture and **pipe** a line along one short end of the Swiss roll tin. Now take the bag containing the chocolate mixture and pipe a line beside the pistachio one leaving a slight gap between the two. Repeat the process, piping alternate lines of pistachio and chocolate mixtures until the tin is filled.

6. Bake both sponges for 17–20 minutes until risen and pale golden. To check that the cakes are cooked, press gently in the centre – they should spring back. Leave to cool in the tins then transfer to a work surface. Wash and dry the round tin ready to assemble the cake.

7. Using a plate or upturned bowl as a guide, cut a 16cm circle out of the round sponge and place in the base of the tin so there's a gap around the edges. Carefully peel away the lining paper from the striped sponge and cut the sponge into two lengthways strips, each 5cm deep. Neaten the ends of one strip and fit into the side of the tin so that the side of the sponge that was papered fits against the tin. Cut the other strip so it fits around the other side of the tin and the ends meet.

To make the chocolate mousse
8. Put the 250g chocolate in a heatproof bowl with the 7 tablespoons double cream and set the bowl over a pan of gently simmering water, making sure the bottom of the bowl doesn't touch the water. Turn off the heat and stir the mixture occasionally so the chocolate melts evenly.
Continued

9. Thoroughly wash one of the mixing bowls and the whisk. Add the 5 egg whites to the bowl and whisk until the whites form soft peaks that flop over when the whisk is lifted. Whisk in the 50g caster sugar. Spoon a quarter of the egg whites into the bowl containing the chocolate and stir in gently until the ingredients are combined. Scrape the rest of the egg whites into the bowl. This time, fold the whites into the chocolate mixture with a large metal spoon until just combined. Turn the mousse into the sponge-lined case and spread level. Chill in the fridge for at least 2 hours or overnight if that suits you better.

To assemble and decorate
10. To finish the pistachio cream, whisk the 100g icing sugar and 75g butter in a bowl until light and creamy. Tip in the ground pistachios and whisk until smooth. Spread the pistachio cream over the top of the chocolate mousse. Once fairly level, texture the surface slightly by running the edge of a palette knife back and forth across the surface. Return to the fridge.

11. To make the chocolate roses, divide the 150g chocolate modelling paste into 15 even-sized pieces. Take one piece and roll it into a thin sausage between the palms of your hands. Flatten out the paste as thinly as you can between your thumb and forefinger. Work along the whole length of the paste until it's about 18cm long. Dust your hands with a little cocoa powder if the paste starts to stick. Starting at one end, roll up the paste loosely to resemble an open rose. Make the remainder in the same way.

12. Transfer the gateau to a serving plate. Arrange the chocolate roses, evenly spaced, around the top edge of the cake.

What pastry or patisserie recipe shall I bake today?

Conversion Table

WEIGHT		VOLUME		LINEAR	
Metric	**Imperial**	**Metric**	**Imperial**	**Metric**	**Imperial**
25g	1oz	30ml	1fl oz	2.5cm	1in
50g	2oz	50ml	2fl oz	3cm	1¼in
75g	2½oz	75ml	3fl oz	4cm	1½in
85g	3oz	125ml	4fl oz	5cm	2in
100g	4oz	150ml	¼ pint	5.5cm	2¼in
125g	4½oz	175ml	6fl oz	6cm	2½in
140g	5oz	200ml	7fl oz	7cm	2¾in
175g	6oz	225ml	8fl oz	7.5cm	3in
200g	7oz	300ml	½ pint	8cm	3¼in
225g	8oz	350ml	12fl oz	9cm	3½in
250g	9oz	400ml	14fl oz	9.5cm	3¾in
280g	10oz	450ml	¾ pint	10cm	4in
300g	11oz	500ml	18fl oz	11cm	4¼in
350g	12oz	600ml	1 pint	12cm	4½in
375g	13oz	725ml	1¼ pints	13cm	5in
400g	14oz	1 litre	1¾ pints	14cm	5½in
425g	15oz			15cm	6in
450g	1lb			16cm	6½in
500g	1lb 2oz			17cm	6½in
550g	1lb 4oz			18cm	7in
600g	1lb 5oz			19cm	7½in
650g	1lb 7oz			20cm	8in
700g	1lb 9oz			22cm	8½in
750g	1lb 10oz			23cm	9in
800g	1lb 12oz			24cm	9½in
850g	1lb 14oz			25cm	10in
900g	2lb				
950g	2lb 2oz				
1kg	2lb 4oz				

SPOON MEASURES

Metric	Imperial
5ml	1 teaspoon
10ml	2 teaspoons
15ml	1 tablespoon
30ml	2 tablespoons
45ml	3 tablespoons
60ml	4 tablespoons
75ml	5 tablespoons

Index

Acknowledgements

Hodder & Stoughton and Love Productions would like to thank the following people for their contribution to this book:

Joanna Farrow, Linda Collister, Laura Herring, Alasdair Oliver, Kate Brunt, Susan Spratt, Joanna Seaton, Sarah Christie, Alice Moore, Nicky Barneby, Anna Heath, Damian Horner, Auriol Bishop, Anna Beattie, Rupert Frisby, Jane Treasure, Claire Emerson.

First published in Great Britain in 2016
by Hodder & Stoughton
An Hachette UK company

1

Copyright © Love Productions Limited 2016
Photography & Design Copyright © Hodder & Stoughton Ltd 2016

Hardback ISBN 978 1 473 61546 5
Ebook ISBN 978 1 473 61547 2

Editorial Director: Nicky Ross
Editor: Sarah Hammond
Project Editor: Laura Herring
Series Editor: Linda Collister
Art Director & Designer: Alice Moore
Photographer: David Munns, Rita Platts
Food Stylist: Joanna Farrow
Props Stylist: Victoria Allen

Typeset in Dear Joe, Mostra, Kings Caslon and Gill Sans
Printed and bound in Italy by L.E.G.O. Spa

Hodder & Stoughton Ltd
Carmelite House
50 Victoria Embankment
London EC4Y 0DZ

www.hodder.co.uk

Continue on your journey to star baker with tips and advice on how to *Bake It Better* from the **GREAT BRITISH BAKE OFF** team.

DON'T JUST BAKE. BAKE IT BETTER.